The question is often asked: why did the Jews not resist the Germans, especially in the face of certain death? The fact is there was organized Jewish resistance. But what is even more remarkable is the fact that the Jews were able to organize any resistance at all.

As the Germans marched through eastern Europe, whole armies of well-trained soldiers were crushed and annihilated by the Nazi war machine. How then were civilians, poorly armed and untrained, supposed to counter the Gestapo and SS? There was no such thing as civil disobedience against the Germans, for civil disobedience requires a "moral" government which will accept protest without inflicting death on innocent and accused alike. Further, the Germans played on the anti-Semitic nature of much of the eastern European non-Jewish population, who, in order to save themselves, were all too eager to help the Germans rid their communities of the *Judenrat*.

Unlike the rest of the civilian population, Jews were faced with the problem of *total* extermination by the Nazis. The dual aim of those Jews who were able to resist the Germans was not only to disrupt the German war effort, but to save as many Jews from extermination as possible.

ESCAPE FROM THE HOLOCAUST

William S. Ruben
&
Paul Ruben

MANOR
BOOKS
INC.

ACKNOWLEDGEMENT

To all those who remembered, some with great pain, some wishing to remain anonymous. And especially to Menachem Warshawski who gave permission to publish his recollections, and to Nacha Katz who painstakingly told our researcher, Alan Winson, so much of what was personal and so much that had to be told. Our thanks, too, to the Yivo Institute, which made heretofore unpublished material available.

Photos: U.S. Army Photographs and from private sources
Photos: Wide World pp. 217, 218, 226

A MANOR BOOK 1978

Manor Books, Inc.
432 Park Avenue South
New York, New York 10016

ISBN CODE 0-532-29102-6

CONTENTS

FOREWORD

In one sense the title of this book is misleading: survivors of the Holocaust cannot escape the memory of those years. Oh, they may have regained liberty or, in some instances, gained it for the first time. Depression comes over so many who are now in their middle years when they are asked to recall the inhumanity and degradation that was forced upon them. For others, the retelling is a form of catharsis as it is for many who listen to the stories, read about them or see visual documentaries and dramatizations. It is impossible in a book of this size to fully describe the enormity of the horror of the days of "The Final Solution." Indeed, it may be impossible to ever accomplish this task. Sadly, the stories of one individual parallel in heartbreaking detail the stories of hundreds of thousands of others. Whose story do you retell? Whose do you omit? Well, there was no attempt to make such a decision. A few were selected, not because the individuals are any more important than others, not because the stories are more dramatic, not because the tellers are more articulate—rather because one suggests many. And these accounts are told, not without some awareness that many of the readers do not come to this book as innocents: they know what happened, if not in detail, in essence.

There is also the matter of history. To retell the chronology of events from the time the National Socialists, with Hitler, came to power in Germany, through to the end of World War II, would only repeat what capable historians have already done. What has been attempted is to integrate the personal stories with history. What happened in the world capitals in the 1930s and '40s was not done in isolation from the Jews and others who suffered by many of those decisions. The Munich pact gave the Germans free rein to move on Poland. The German/Soviet non-aggression agreement squeezed the Polish Jews to extinction. The British and American interests in the Mid-East argued against total participation in helping Jews escape from Europe. These are not absolutes. There were exceptions, many. But the facts of history are not mere statistics for students to remember and repeat by rote. History is of the dead and the tortured, but history is also of the living.

A Nacha or Menachem or Bernard tells his or her story, sometimes after being assured that the listener is willing to tell the truth. That was the primary requisite, to tell the truth. No one who was not subject to the Nazi terror can truly feel what they and others lived through. Pictures of death camps are often regarded as grotesque picture postcards. There is a sympathetic ear and then, on to other matters. Sure, that's as it should be. The future is for the living. But for those who lived through the years of the Holocaust, the future is for not forgetting. A woman momentarily comes out of years of depression as she warms to recounting the awesome years. A man recalls that he might have been a doctor and now drives a taxi and remembers.

So many have planned to write, to talk. But they can only think and sleep less, disturbed by recurring nightmares. If some of these stories are told awkwardly by the survivors, it is because there was no sense of humane reason to what happened to them. They reflected that. But the stories are true. The pictures are real. And, in some small way, it is hoped this book will help the future profit from the past.   WSR & PR
New York, May 1978

ONE

THIS IS THE LAW
OF THE BURNT OFFERING...

In the earliest of Jewish rituals the high priest would symbolically lay upon a goat the sins of all of his people. Then the animal would be cast out into the wilderness. This act, performed on what would be called the Day of Atonement, "shall be an everlasting statute unto you, to make an atonement for the children of Israel for all their sins once a year" as it was written in Leviticus XVI. And so, to this day, one who innocently is caused to bear the burden of iniquity for a guilty party is called a scapegoat. In 1933 it was an articulated fact that the

German Chancellor, Adolf Hitler, with his professed dislike for Jews, had made them his chosen scapegoat. Whether he would cast them out into the wilderness or cause them to be sacrificed was still unknown.

The prestigious U.S. radio commentator H.V. Kaltenborn had, along with other Western journalists, requested a personal interview with Hitler. For what reason the German Chancellor changed his policy concerning meeting with the Western press is not fully understood. But, after a careful check of Kaltenborn's credentials, an appointment was arranged outside of Munich in Hitler's summer home. Hitler's views on Jews was to be a prime topic of the meeting.

That Hitler thought Kaltenborn would serve as a conduit for his own propaganda is entirely possible. Early on Hitler appreciated the power of the press, the effect of his own oratory and persuasion. Nevertheless, it was a journalistic coup for the American. But how the world would react to the information he would bring back was a matter of history.

The German leader was to the point. The Jews of Germany were an internal affair. He told Kaltenborn:

"We have no concern with the Jews of other lands, but we are very much concerned about the anti-German elements within our country. We demand the right to deal with these elements as we see fit. Jews have been the intellectual proponents of subversive anti-German movements, and as such they must be dealt with."

No one outside Germany in 1933 could have known or even predicted the full meaning of Hitler's words, "...to deal with these elements as we see fit." The ordeal, the unparalleled horror Eastern European Jews suffered from 1933-1945 in Nazi Germany, could not be imagined by that radio commentator or anyone else in the world.

Many scholars argue that the destruction of the Jews was not planned; that, after Hitler came to power in 1933, the machinery of genocide against the Jews grew through the network of offices in the Nazi party, out of the economic conditions, social attitudes and general anti-Semitism prevalent among a good many German people. Many others insist that as early as Hitler was capable of remembering, he wanted to somehow rid the world of all Jews. Both sentiments are true. And both sentiments ultimately led to the Final Solution: the total extermination of all Jews in Europe.

Those who knew Hitler as a youth confirm his early anti-Jewish attitudes. By the time he went to Vienna as a young man, Hitler was a confirmed anti-Semite. Failing to achieve any personal success he grew more and more preoccupied with "Jews" while living in the Austrian capital, which out of its two million inhabitants had nearly 200,000 Jews.

In his prophetic work *Mein Kampf* Hitler tells a story about walking one day through Vienna's inner city. Hitler recalls he suddenly encountered a ghost "in a black caftan and black sidelocks. Is this a Jew?" was his first thought. Hitler stared in disbelief that this could *also* be a German. Impossible, he thought.

Hitler read a score of anti-Semitic books shortly after the incident to confirm his belief that Jews were not like the rest of society. He returned to the inner city again to look at these Jews cloaked in black. "Wherever I went," wrote Hitler, "I began to see Jews, and the more I saw, the more sharply they became distinguished in my eyes from the rest of humanity...Later I often grew sick to the stomach from the smell of these caftan-wearers."

Hitler equated Jews with all that was wrong with society. He blamed them for everything, from the moral decay of Vienna to organized prostitution, to the seduction of unknowing Christian girls in order to adulterate their blood. He wrote of the "nightmare vision of the seduction of hundreds of thousands of girls by repulsive, crooked-legged Jew bastards."

By the time Hitler moved to Germany for good in 1913, he was consumed with an absolute hatred for Jews. As he later wrote, "Gradually, I began to hate them." Referring to his early youth, he continued, "I had ceased to be a weak-kneed cosmopolitan and became and anti-Semite."

Throughout his life and until the end in a Berlin bunker Hitler blamed the Jews for literally everything that was wrong with Germany. Hitler's fanatical anger against the Jews made Germany the first country in the history of mankind to wage a massive campaign of genocide which would include six million Jews and almost an equal number of Poles, Russians and others.

The roots of racism against the Jews did not begin with the birth of Adolf Hitler. Not just Germans, but non-Jews around the world regarded Jewish people as those who rejected the Redeemer, Jesus, and thus had condemned themselves to ostracism and eternal distrust of the Christian world.

It wasn't until the De Ecclesia of the Second Vatican Council that the words "perfidious Jews" were removed from the liturgy. That Hitler could seize upon the Jews as a scapegoat for the loss of World War I and the subsequent economic upheaval in Germany was no surprise. But that he could enter upon such a concerted and controlled elimination of the Jews of his country without the rest of the world either knowing about it or if knowing, reacting, is surprising.

After World War I, the German state was in a chaotic condition; politically, economically and morally. Many Germans simply refused to accept the fact that they'd been beaten, yet their country was forced to accept the strict war reparations, the restrictions of the Versailles Treaty placed upon them by the victorious allies.

The postwar Weimar Republic did not challenge the Allied demand for huge war repayments, which the German people considered excessive punishment. A weak government, rampant inflation, a ceaseless near-paranoiac fear of communism, made it possible for Hitler, his burgeoning National Socialist Party, and racism to grow.

It was as early as 1924 when the Nazis began openly calling for a solution to the "Jewish problem." At the time, most of the population regarded these fanatics as little more than right-wing freaks. Still, the Nazis were able to introduce anti-Jewish legislation in the Reichstag. Raving lunatic proposals, they failed terribly in 1924. But ten years later they would become the law of the land.

As Hitler rapidly ascended to power, his need to find a scapegoat which the German people could focus on as the root of their problems grew. Hitler's venom for the Jews billowed in the late twenties and early thirties as his Nazi Party not only preached that Jews were economically destructive to German interests (accusing them of conspiring against Germany with the economic institutions they controlled) but that Jews were *inherently* subhuman and evil.

In 1928, when the Nazi Party could barely capture 3% of the vote in national elections, Germans were being told by this fringe group that the German people constituted the highest stratum of the Nordic-Aryan race. Jews, a sub-human race, were continually trying to infect the Aryans with their "perverted" Jewish blood. Jews, the Germans were told, would undermine the government and German people with their liberal/communist philosophy.

In 1930, in the midst of a world depression, the Nazis gained dramatically in the Reichstag, capturing 18% of the votes and 107 seats. They continued to pour out their anti-Semitic message.

Jews, said the Nazis, should be separated from the rest of society. They were not, as some professed, part of humanity. Rather, they were a totally different race, whose ultimate goal was the destruction of the Aryan people and domination of the world.

By 1933 the Weimar Republic was in complete disarray. Changes in government occurred frequently. Although the Nazi faction, led by Hitler, was a minority party, those who wanted to exploit Hitler's popularity (and assumed weakness as a leader) helped vault him to Chancellor in 1933. Hitler, however, was not to be used. His supporters soon found that *he* was using them for his own ends.

Almost immediately, Hitler used his new rank as a platform to 'legally' prevent Jews from participating in government and society. Three months after his appointment as Chancellor (in March of 1933) Hitler established Germany's first concentration camp at Dachau. At the time, Dachau was used as a prison for all dissenters, most of whom were *not* Jews. The feared Gestapo, which Hitler formed in April of 1933, usually sent political prisoners (including all suspected communists, socialists, liberals, and ordinary Germans who

"Be hard, be ruthless, act more quickly and brutally than others. This is the most humanitarian method of warfare because it frightens people...And now forward — against the enemy!"
(A. Hitler, 8.22.39)

Sept. 4, 1939, Silesia. Immediately after invading Poland, the

Nazis began mass arrests and executions.

Mass arrests of residents of Piotrkow Trybunalski.

Soldiers blindfold women brought to the execution site.

Those arrested were thrown into the torture chambers of the Gestapo prisons, shot, or sent to concentration camps.

opposed the Nazi policy of violence) to Dachau where they were routinely terrorized, beaten and killed. In actual fact, it wasn't until several years later that masses of Jews were sent to camps like Dachau. But by the end of 1933, Hitler had created approximately 50 concentration camps.

1933 began the first stage of official German anti-Semitism. German people were exhorted to boycott Jewish businesses. Hitler publicly declared that Jews were not Germans. On April 1, 1933 he proclaimed a national boycott of all Jewish shops. On that day armed guards (mostly members of the SS) picketed Jewish-owned factories and shops. Demonstrations were urged to show support for Hitler's national program.

Violence became the order of the day. Although Hitler had not yet publicly called for Jewish extermination, thousands of Jews were robbed, beaten, and murdered, as the brown-shirted police looked on.

It is often said that freedom is indivisible, that civil liberties are not something to be doled out. It is equally true that to deprive a man of his freedom in one aspect of his life is to deprive him of all of his freedom. What happened in the early 1930s would be magnified with succeeding years.

In the summer of 1934 Adolf Hitler would tell a completely subdued and cowering Reichstag, following a Nazi purge of dissidents, "The Supreme Court of the German People during these twenty-four hours consisted of myself!"

The ineffectual and defeated Hindenburg had died. The Nazis had assassinated Chancellor Dollfuss of

Austria. The Western world noted and reported the events, but little else. If there was concern in the rest of the world, it was isolated and mostly unheard. It wasn't until 1937 that James F. Byrnes (who would later be elevated to the U.S. Supreme Court), as a delegate to the Inter-Parliamentary Union in Paris, decided to investigate Europe's economic problems. The German Foreign Office arranged for Byrnes to attend the Annual Congress of the Nazi Party. He would write years later in *Speaking Frankly,* "I had watched the rise of this man Hitler with a somewhat detached concern, but here was a scene that could not be regarded with detachment.... What was spread before us, however, was a program not for economic recovery but for armed aggression. Twelve thousand troops marched past our stand accompanied by the rumble of scores of tanks and motorized weapons, while 450 planes swept across the skies above the stadium. As the demonstration reached its climax, Hitler rode across the field in an open automobile, standing erect and with right arm uplifted in the Nazi salute. An exultant cry arose from the multitude. But I was frightened—frightened by the specter of war."

What Byrnes did not see and was not shown was what was behind the ubiquitous German posters with the slogan "Joy Through Work." The total destruction of the Jews had begun four years earlier.

What was it like to be a Jew in Germany? What was it like to be a Jew wherever Hitler's soldiers marched and conquered? David P. Boder, then Director of the Psychological Museum of Chicago, recorded an interview with an Abraham K., who was born in Upper Silesia in Poland in 1928. His early encounters with

German oppression came about during the conquest of Poland. What Byrnes did not see less than five years earlier, what the world did not concern itself with was now directly confronting young Abraham. As the Germans approached his home near the frontier he fled with thousands of others. After a week of hiding there was no place to go. He told the interviewer: "Seven days after the Germans came in we decided to return because they were everywhere. What could we do? And when we came near Swaskow, that is a little village also not far from us...we heard that all the Jews have been thrown from the bridge into the water. And that is the real truth. When they saw a Jew, that time one was still recognizable because the religious Jews still wore their beards and they were dressed in Jewish fashion...And when it was a Jew they either shot him or threw him into the water alive..."

Abraham, along with thousands of other Jews, would either work for the Germans or die. The sick, the old, the children were summarily executed. But what may seem incongruous is that many of the old, knowing they faced death, refused to hide. There is no rational explanation. The Germans asked Jewish leaders to calm the populace, that their transporation to Auschwitz was nothing to fear.

Jews were asked to sign confessions that they were criminals and would accept their sentence to Auschwitz. Who was a criminal? One who did not properly attach the Star of David Jews were required to wear. He or she was a criminal. A Jew who did not walk in the prescribed area was a criminal.

German Task Forces made periodic raids, rounding up Jews. Young Abraham was young and apparently strong and working well for the Germans. He would survive the raids, the concentration camps, the horror. In his own words, after learning that he, too, was destined to be rounded up, "...I was told that they came looking for me. I became completely perplexed. My blood stopped functioning when they told me that...I had courage and was always imagining the worst..."

He was afraid to be separated from his mother and sister, more than the fear of death. The Germans had come to his home looking for him. The Germans were precise, formal, almost apologetic. He was found and, because he was young, was sent to a work camp, forced to run the eight kilometers, guarded by soldiers and dogs. And much later Abraham recounted how those who could not run stopped and waited to be shot by the guards. He told of men with full senses, but physically weak, waiting by the roadside to die. Every ten to thirty yards a body would be thrown into a ditch. Twelve thousand men were marched from Markstadt to Gross-Rosen. Nearly eight thousand perished or were slaughtered along the route. Abraham is confused as to the exact numbers. But the picture he remembers is clear, "...when we got up in the morning the dead were stapled like railroad ties..."

Abraham was to be sent to a work camp at Dulag. "We had to run (there) about eight kilometers." They were guarded by soldiers and dogs, which were fed before the prisoners. "They would say, when they shoot a Jew they have one bread left over and they could feed a dog."

Work in camp was more than labor: it was a test of cunning, of scavenging food, of enduring beatings for infractions of rules which restricted an inmate's most basic needs. "When one was beaten...one has to remain lying for a moment; they would take advantage of the situation and continue beating him...After the beating they would let you loose, but you couldn't get up..." The crime, taking three turnips.

Escape is survival. Survival is cunning. Endurance is luck. "Those who had no 'luck' and had to live only from their rations, they just didn't survive..."

Ordinary criminals were imprisoned with Jews and they became their executioners. It may have been because Abraham was young and healthy that he survived the beatings, that he endured the hunger, outwitted his captors. It may have been that he survived because he was of use to the Germans, who would kill a worker whose feet were swollen.

German garbage became reservoirs of strength for those who could forage in them unnoticed. The obscenity of the 'dead room' was unreal. He was beaten much and fed little and would be kept alive as long as he was able to work. Prisoners were permitted to be beaten, if they could return to work. They had to march in strict formation. Laggards were no better off than the infirm. Death through beatings and starvation and extermination were so common than one in three prisoners had a 'life' expectancy of perhaps three months. The young boy saw older men wait for the SS men to kill them, men with their minds alert even though their bodies were no longer capable of movement. When the men were rested they would literally kill for a place to sleep. They had no beds, no plans, no food. They performed their bodily functions where they lay, where they were frozen into immobility. But he survived. Was it by some unknown chance? Was it through courage, faith? Why this one and not that one? Why?

To what heights or depths would the Germans go. It

was thought by those few who survived the first days of Hitler in 1933 that the Nazi anti-Jewish policy had already reached unprecedented heights.

On the seventh day of April, 1933 German Jews learned for the first time that they were being systematically denied their civil rights. Jews who worked for the government found they were no longer accepted. Jews who wanted to work in government found they would not be hired.

LAW FOR THE RESTORATION OF THE PROFESSIONAL CIVIL SERVICE
April 7, 1933

The Reich Government has enacted the following law, promulgated herewith:
...civil servants may be dismissed from office in accordance with the regulations that follow, even in the absence of the conditions required therefor under present law.
3 (1) Civil servants who are not of Aryan descent are to be retired (§ §8 ff); if they are honorary officials, they are to be dismissed from official status.

The Nazis continued their efforts to exclude Jews from all aspects of German life.

The playing of German composer Mendelssohn was banned. He was a Jew. The music of Germany's leading composer, Paul Hindemith, was strictly *verboten*. Soon Jews were taken out of great symphony orchestras and the opera.

In May of 1933 books published by Jewish authors were burned. The "Reich Press Law of October 4, 1933," which made journalism a 'public vocation,' regulated by law, said that all editors must be German citizens, be of Aryan descent and not be married to a Jew.

The *Vossische Zeitung,* one of Germany's leading newspapers (founded in 1704 and comparable to the *London Times* and *New York Times),* went out of business in April of 1934. The paper was owned by the House of Ullstein, a Jewish firm.

The Nazi government prohibited Jews from practicing law:

LAW REGARDING ADMISSION TO THE BAR

The Reich government has enacted the following law herewith:

1. The admission to the bar of lawyers who, according to the Law for the Restoration of the Professional Civil Service of April 7, 1933 (Reichsgesetzblatt I, p.175), are of non-Aryan descent may be revoked until September 30, 1933.

By the end of 1933 it was apparent that German Jewry was being isolated from the rest of the Republic. Hitler ordered German scientists to investigate what he called 'race science,' a theory used to prove "scientifically" that Jews were an inferior race.

Because most Jews were accepted members of society (if not always thought highly of) prior to the Third Reich, and because they represented only 1% of the German population (500,000; a third of whom lived in Berlin) it was difficult to accept such rapid and total disaffection.

Prior to Hitler's regime, German Jews tended to be politically middle of the road, generally non-Zionist and essentially of German heritage. They were Germans first, Jews second. The Jewish people were an integral part of the German political, social, cultural and economic fabric. To most of them Nazism was only another anti-Semitic aberration.

Before 1934 representatives of various Jewish factions (including Zionists, orthodox, non-Zionists) met to help discuss their future. Most decided to keep within their own circles, hoping that if they remained apart from the rest of society, Hitler would leave them alone. But two historical incidents occurred which forever would prevent the Jews from living peacefully, even amongst themselves; On December 1, 1933, Hitler declared the legal unity of the German State and Nazi Party. Very simply, anti-Semitism became national policy. In August of 1934, President Hindenburg (who was by now virtually powerless) died. Hitler, who had been waiting in the wings for full, unchallenged power, became Head of State and Commander-in-Chief of the armed forces.

As 1934 progressed, the clouds continually darkened over German Jewry. It was not yet *official* policy to deport or kill Jews; their separation from the rest of German society continued. In May of that year, Dr. Joseph Goebbels, Hitler's propaganda minister, warned German Jews not to tread upon the Third Reich. In a speech he made on May 11, 1934, Geobbels admonished the Jews:

"We have been very lenient with the Jews. But if they think that therefore they can still be allowed on German stages, offering art to the German people,...writing for German newspapers...they might take these words as a final warning. Jewry can rest assured that we will leave them alone as long as they retire quietly...as long as they are not provocative and do not affront the German people with the claim to be treated as equals. If the Jews do not listen to this warning, they will have themselves to blame for anything that happens to them."

From this point on Jews found themselves ostracized from businesses, community groups, even entire towns and villages.

On May 26, 1934 the German district of Hersbruck publicly announced with pride that it had 'purged' its district of all Jews. In a public notice, the district party leader, Comrade Sperber, was credited with educating the citizens of his community to the dangers of letting Jewish citizens live in the district. "We are firmly convinced," the notice went on to read, "that other districts will soon follow suit, and that the day is not now far off when throughout the whole of Germany there will no longer be one single Jew."

By 1935 thousands of Jews were being imprisoned, charged with little more than being a Jew. Many had already realized the ultimate danger of Nazism and had made their way out of Germany to England, America and other countries. By the summer of 1935 posted signs outside village borders were not uncommon. *"Juden Verboten,"* they read.

Jewish businesses were marked with the Star of David, or simply with the letters, *JUDE*. Professionals, doctors, lawyers and others were harassed and arrested, making it impossible for the German Jewish citizen to have any recourse, medical or legal.

Earlier in 1934 the German Jewish newspaper *"Judische Rundschau,"* published an article entitled,

"Wear the Yellow Badge with Pride." It told German Jews to proudly say yes to the Star of David and their heritage. But pro-Jewish slogans would only add a false sense of security to those who remained in Germany.

By 1935 most of the world was perhaps vaguely aware of the German attitude toward Jews. Hitler denied racism. But that didn't prevent boycotts of Nazi Germany by the American Jewish Congress and other foreign groups.

In 1935, the United States, among other nations, was in no mood to overly antagonize the Germans, or anyone else for that matter.

In September of 1935 the German Reichstag would change unalterably the lives of German Jews. In that month, the German government passed a series of laws which spelled out the beginning of doom for all German Jews. It was truly the beginning of the Holocaust, from which few would escape.

TWO

BROKEN DREAMS AND BROKEN GLASS

In the Autumn of 1939 the present Nacha Katz, now living and working in Westchester County, New York, waited with her young husband for the Germans to overrun her Polish town. In 1977 she recalls with some nervousness, some residual anxiety what happened that year. When did the war begin? When the war came to Shblitzika in Poland. She was engaged to be married. It is something to plan for a life ahead, to think of marriage and children and possibly a home of one's own. It is something to plan these common enough events. It is another matter to see the soldiers come into your home town and round up your friends and relatives, to feel the fear, a fear so intense it becomes unreal. The first thing the Germans did "was to take out the elders, the educators, the Zionists, the Jewish leaders. They took them out of town somewhere, made them dig their own graves, took off their clothes and shot them."

Nacha's new husband was to die in a concentration camp. The boy she had known since childhood would never know a fruitful manhood. The cries of Hail Victory to one man became cries of pain and anguish for the conquered. If the Task Force soldiers and the SS were symbols of fear and death to an outside world, to Nacha it was the "whole damn nation." They were the German soldiers she saw coming into her small town. They brought pigs into the synagogue, "made a pig sty of our beautiful building, one which architects would come to admire."

Inteviewing survivors of the Holocaust one wonders at the inconsistencies of what had happened. Why was this one permitted to live, that one to move about, that one to be questioned and tortured, this one to be given food and another to be left to starve? When the Germans came into Nacha's community their first object of destruction was the synagogue. She recalls that, after the burning, they cleaned it out and made the young men, including Nacha's brother, go into the ruins. The soldiers wanted to burn them. "Everybody was standing outside and moaning. Why did we let the men go in? They didn't know what was going to happen to them. But there was nothing left to burn."

The Germans cut off the food supply. But she and others scrounged food from neighboring villages. She could still move about. She would hear a shot and knew someone was executed. She saw the Germans burn their books. She saw the German soldiers swagger. "They went into the streets and shot people, just for pleasure."

That is some of what Nacha remembers: the pleasure of

death and the burning and the way those who had once lived normal lives took the signs of death with a measure of food that could be stolen or bartered. She saw young men herded away and yet she was allowed to move about.

What would provoke a soldier to kill a friend or a neighbor? "Nothing. If I had been in a particular spot at a particular time I would be killed. As I think about it and live it over I know I was not in the wrong place, where they would come, and so I lived. They took, first a few Jews, then the whole city. They took four men, I remember, to a nearby lake and drowned them, little by little. They didn't want them to live, because this was their pleasure. They, the soldiers, stood there, with their guns and laughed.

"I recall there were six or eight of us living in one room. It was now near Christmas 1939. Strangers lived together because there was no place else for them. There was a black market. One man, who my aunt allowed to live with us, gave us a few pounds of meat. Then, one night two German soldiers came in. They had been tipped off. They found the man who had traded in meat and broke their rifles on him. They hit the other men who were there. They hit and hit. I was a teen-ager. I was playing with my cousin and we saw the hitting and we watched and could do nothing. And why did the Germans start? I don't know. But finally somebody came in, a man who knew those Germans or had been dealing with them, and gave them the equivalent of a few dollars. They took the money and left. And only the swollen, broken bodies of the men remained.

"The Germans would come again and say to the mothers, 'Give us your children!' "

Nacha hesitated, went on, "They come in to you and

you have to give them your child. The women were told to bring their children to one central place and they thought their children would be inoculated. They took the children away, babies, three and four years old. They killed them!"

If Nacha could provide no reason for the provocation, the essence of the German soldiers' motivation was firmly imprinted. The law of the land had been laid down by the leaders years before.

By the summer of 1935 the German Reichstag was virtually a rubber stamp law-making body for Adolf Hitler. Along with General Hermann Wilhelm Goering, Hitler prepared to *legally* separate Jewish and gentile German citizens. It was simply a matter of telling the Reichstag *what* the law would be.

In 1935, according to Hitler (at least in theory), German Jews should be afforded the same rights (though not privileges) as non-Jews. In other words, Jews would be considered legally separate, but equal. In September of that year, Hitler decreed Jews would be afforded the same legal protection as Aryan citizens. However, a second law which he created stated that *only* Aryan citizens could aspire to the honorary rank of "Citizen of the Reich."

Very carefully, Hitler placed in the minds of Germans the notion that Jews and non-Jews should not mix. To strengthen that belief, and to provide a *legal* groundwork for the ultimate disappearance of Jewish Germans, Chancellor Hitler introduced at the same time the "Nuremberg Laws."

Two basic laws (accompanied by a series of regulations governing their implementation) dramatically altered the

Mass executions of civilians in Poland.

In June 1940, the Nazis shot Polish patriots near Warsaw.
The victims were beaten up, then blindfolded and their

mouths covered with plaster of paris. Then they were shot
by firing squads from a distance of 6 ft. 6 in.

More executions by firing squad.

Men and women conducted to execution site and shot right over open graves.

"Pacification" of the village of Cycow during which its inhabitants were shot.

Old men and women with children in their arms were shot after digging their own graves.

In the early years, hanging executions abounded. Sometimes, smiling Nazi officers posed in front of gallows.

Civilians, including young girls and pregnant women, were hanged on makeshift gallows.

A public execution in the market square in Lodz in 1941.

course of Jewish history in Germany. The first, called the "Reich Citizenship Law," decreed that only persons "of German blood" (Aryans) could be citizens of the Reich. All persons of "impure blood," that is non-Aryans, would not be regarded as citizens, but rather as "subjects." For the first time in their history, German Jews were told that "legally" they *were not* German citizens.

The second law was even more devastating to the security of the Jewish population. Called the "Law for the Protection of German Blood and Honor," it was decreed that:

1. Marriages between Jews and German citizens are forbidden. Such marriages contracted in spite of the law, even if performed in a foreign country, would not be recognized by the Third Reich.
2. Extra-marital relations between Jews and Germans are forbidden.
3. The employment in Jewish households of German mid-servants under the age of 45 is forbidden.

Violators of these and other related regulations were punished with long and often severe prison terms.

German Jewry's immediate response to the Nuremberg Laws was a combination of wish and hope. Many Jews thought that, once separated from society, they would be left alone. In a number of speeches, Hitler said as much. Besides, many Jews felt that their economic contribution to Germany was indispensable for its growth. This, of course, was an unfortunate delusion. The fact was the Nuremberg Laws left Jews virtually defenseless in their own land. They couldn't legally fight an eviction from a job, seizure of their property, or even get redress.

After the passage of the Nuremberg Laws, there was some question as to what constituted a "Jew."

Hitler was extremely concerned about mixing the races. According to an estimate made by Rudolf Hess in 1936, Germany had nearly half a million full, three-quarter, or one-half Jews, plus another 300,000 who fell into the category "Jewish *Mischling*" (roughly translated, *Mischling* means one with blood from both races). Hitler felt it necessary that the Jewish *Mischling* not be excluded from the Nuremberg Laws, no matter how little Jewish blood they possessed.

Making it impossible for anyone of non-Jewish blood to consort with someone with even a small amount of Jewish blood helped establish the basis of the final legal/biological solution to the Jewish problem. The official commentary to the Nuremberg Laws makes this plain; "The aim of a legal solution to the *Mischling* question must be the disappearance of the *Mischling* race."

The Nazis assumed that German Jewry would be extinct within a matter of two generations. The problem of hidden Jews (that is those with mixed blood) would also be eliminated.

The German leaders made certain that Jews could not work with or for Aryans by requiring potential employees to submit proof of ancestry. In point of fact, a young German man wishing to join Himmler's racially elite SS had to offer evidence of Aryan ancestry that could be traced back to 1750.

The Nuremberg Laws brought to a close the legal phase of Nazi Jewish policy. German Jews could read dispassionately the law of the land; a law which made them officially second-class citizens. Or they could listen to the passionate German leaders extolling the necessity of separate Jewish legislation. Hermann Goering, who would commit suicide rather than face trial as a war criminal, was called upon to justify the anti-Jewish laws:

> "We must preserve the Germanic and Nordic purity of the race, and must protect our women and girls with every means...In this pure blood stream will blossom forth a new era of Germanic happiness. Every Nazi German finds in his race and in his people the highest fulfillment of his individual being, and is ready to give up his whole life for both."

Apparently most of the German Jews, despite the proscriptions of the National Socialist Party, still could not consider Germany anything except their home. What was to come was either never understood or, if so, not believed. Nevertheless it is estimated that in the year the Nuremberg Laws were enacted about 78,000 Jews left the country. In the next three years little more than double that number were able to get out of the country.

By the time war broke out Hitler's *Final Solution* was not confined to German Jews but to Jews wherever his armies conquered. But until that time, unbelievably, there were still Jews in Germany who thought they might be able to survive or perhaps just endure Hitler's Third Reich.

The passage of anti-Jewish laws was not enough to satisfy Hitler's overwhelming hate for that segment of German society. The German Jews left in Germany could have lived peacefully with their separate, second-class status.

In March of 1938, eight months after the opening of the Buchenwald concentration camp, Germany marched across the Austrian border, making that separate territory part of the German Reich. Austria's Jewish population was literally uprooted by the Nazi occupation force. In what William L. Shirer described as "an orgy of sadism," Jews were plucked from their jobs and homes, and forced to work on their hands and knees for jeering storm troopers. Thousands were jailed. Everything they owned was confiscated and stolen. Squads of German soldiers could be seen carrying away valuables of Austrian Jews. It is estimated that nearly half of Vienna's 180,000 Jews were still able to *buy* their freedom to emigrate by giving over their possessions to the Nazis. The SS formed a special organization to handle this process called the "Office For Jewish Emigration." It was administered by one of Hitler's close friends; an Austrian Nazi named Karl Adolf Eichmann. Eventually this agency came to work not for Jewish emigration, but Jewish extermination.

Life for German Jews in 1937 and 1938 rapidly declined. Mass arrests increased. The burning and looting of Jewish shops and synagogues was accelerated. On October 5, 1938, passports held by Jews were invalidated. Jews who were permitted them in order to emigrate were given passports stamped with the letter "J" (which stood for *"Jude"*).

In that same year Polish Jews were expelled en masse and since Poland refused to accept them, they were forced to live near the frontier area in the most intolerable of conditions. They belonged to no country, were subject to no protection, to no law except the one of persecution.

With Jews being expelled from each country occupied by the Wehrmacht, they needed a place to go. Most other nations would not accept them. In July of 1938 President Roosevelt convened the Evian Conference in France. The conference was designed to bring relief to displaced Jews.

However, most free nations stood firmly against Jewish emigration into their own countries. Only the British mandate of Palestine was available. But this the British fought, the political complexities of the Near East being no less then than they are today.

It was in 1917 Arthur James Balfour, the British Foreign Secretary, had written Lord Rothschild, then head of the British Zionist Party: "His Majesty's Government view with favor the establishment in Palestine of a national home for the Jewish people, and will use their best endeavors to facilitate the achievement of this object, it being clearly understood that nothing shall be done that may prejudice the civil and religious rights of existing non-Jewish communities in Palestine, or the rights and political status enjoyed by Jews in any other country."

Nevertheless, despite, or perhaps because of, the enunciation of this 'declaration', Menachem Begin would have added to his enemies list the British government. It is possible that with the death of his mentor, Jabotinsky, compounded by his own arrest and imprisonment the Begin who was the fiery orator was metamorphosed into the Begin who would brook no compromise, who would be unyielding and demanding in his idea of what territory should comprise the new Jewish State. The motto of the Irgun, one of whose basic goals was to rid Palestine of the British, was "Judea collapsed in fire and blood. Judea will rise in fire and blood."

It is of more than just mere historical interest to put in perspective the political climate in Poland, German aggression and the beginnings of the formation of the present State of Israel. The present Prime Minister of Israel, Menachem Begin, came out of that climate. What happens today is, to a great extent, conditioned by the Holocaust. To forget the impression it made on any of the survivors is to do a disservice to human dignity. To disregard the impression it has made on men of authority is to disregard the events of history.

Thirty-seven years after his arrest by the Russians Menachem Begin told William E. Farrell of *The New York Times,* "I was ready to be arrested by the Soviets because, as I said at the grave of a member of the Betar, 'If we can't fight for our country, then we shall suffer for it.' It was an hour of hopelessness. So I preferred to go to prison ...Indeed when they came to arrest me, I was almost a happy man." What led up to his arrest in Poland, what made this man an object of persecution by the N.K.V.D., the Russian secret police, is tied into anti-Semitism in Poland, the rise of Hitler and, not least of all, the particular intelligence and charismatic qualities of Menachem Wolfovitch Begin.

The present Prime Minister of Israel was born in Brest-Litovsk, Poland in 1913. This is the same city in which the Russians gave in to German demands and signed a treaty which abandoned Poland, Lithuania, the Ukraine, the Baltic provinces, Transcaucasia and Finland. By October of 1918 Poland declared war against the Ukraine, eventually recapturing Vilna and advancing into White Russia. By 1920 Poland was strong enough (with support from the French) to demand, and get, most of the territories lost to Russia. Hostility with both Germany and Russia continued, as well as with the various Baltic States. In fact a state of war was in existence between Poland and Lithuania until 1927.

Not only was Begin born into a country beset by war on virtually all its borders but was deeply disturbed within.

Anti-Semitism was, if not a part of government policy, allowed to continue to most abusive proportions. Jews in Poland had no choice but to defend themselves physically and philosophically. There is no question that Begin was active both ways. As a youngster he was influenced by the founder of the Zionist-Revisionist movement, Vladimir Jabotinsky, a Russian Jew. His organization, which some considered a more radical rival to the World Zionist Organization, set as one of its goals in 1925, the establishment of a Jewish State in Palestine. In the light of current history Jabotinsky, a man to whom Begin owes his political indoctrination, demanded that this state be established on both sides of the Jordan River.

Begin had, as a youth, begun a classical education and had begun to study law. But these studies gave way to his virtually total involvement with the Zionist-Revisionist movement. This activity was not only in opposition to Polish government policy, but was putting him in conflict with the Russians and, of course, with the Nazis who had come to power in Germany. But he was also in philosophic disagreement with other Jewish organizations.

Begin had gone to Czechoslovakia to talk on behalf of the Zionist-Revisionist movement. By the Spring of 1938 the Czechs, ever fearful of invasion by the Germans, returned territory to Poland which had been taken during the 1920 Polish-Russian War. After the Munich agreement Poland sided with Hungary in further claims against Czechoslovakia. Nevertheless in March of 1939 Germany made absolute demands on Poland for certain rail rights and annexation of territories including Danzig. These were rejected and the German attack on Poland took place on September 1, 1939.

What Menachem Begin had continued to participate in was the political and social conflict in Poland and Czechosolvakia. Concepts of both the nature of the government and human rights had made Jews in general and those who were activists objects of persecution, arrest, imprisonment and death. The number of Jews were relatively small percentages of the population of most of the Eastern countries. What Begin was aware of in a very pragmatic way was what Salo Baron, a recognized authority on Jewish history, wrote in *A Social and Religious History of the Jews,* "Throughout its history anti-Semitic propaganda frequently proved most virulent in areas of slight Jewish population density. What was attacked was the prevailing image of the Jew rather than any particular Jewish acquaintances whom one could regard as favorable exceptions."

After Stalin and Hitler had signed their abortive non-aggression pact, Foreign Minister Molotov told the Supreme Soviet on October 31, 1939, "...One swift blow to Poland, first by the German and then by the Red Army, and nothing was left of this ugly offspring of the Versailles Treaty..."

And even today, nobody knows for sure how many hundreds of thousands, and perhaps millions, of Poles were shipped as prisoners to the Soviet Union. The Soviet government was deliberately assisting in the decimation and destruction of Poland. In his preaching the cause of the Zionist-Revisionist movement Menachem Begin did nothing to add to the meaning of his first name, which translates as 'comforter.' His avowedly right-wing group was considered fascist by David Ben-Gurion who would become Israel's first Premier. The Russians considered him an enemy of the State. To the Germans he was a Jew and intellectual, either being reason enough for his death. But the Germans were the immediate enemy and it was while he was in hiding in Lithuania that Begin was arrested by the Russians—for being a Zionist.

All Jews were not, of course, political activists, concerned with anything more than the immediate problem of survival. For the Polish Jews this became increasingly remote. The middle-aged Nacha remembers the young teen-ager in Poland, how the slaughter crept up on them. There were many, unlike Begin, who could not fight with their minds or their bodies. They didn't know how to fight. They knew how to endure. And when the German soldiers came in and demanded all their possessions they gave them.

Let Nacha continue her remembrances:

"They come in to say you have to give away all the money. Then, they would come back later and say they want all the furs. If you own any silver, candlesticks or anything of silver or gold and they would find it in your home, your whole family would be shot. So you give everything away. And we would say to ourselves, 'We will manage without them.'

"We weren't rich people. We had no silver. The first thing the Jewish women did was to save the *lichte,* the candles we would light on the Sabbath. We had a few candlesticks, so we buried them in the cellar. These are what we saved, the *tallith,* the *tefillin,* the *lichte.* We would hide them as we hid ourselves.

"We couldn't practice our religion, of course, If the Germans catch you, they shoot you! We could pray in our own house when we knew they were not coming. But there were no synagogues. We never gave up praying. A

Women members of the Jewish Fighters Organization.

ON APRIL 19, 1944, THE INHABITANTS OF THE WARSAW GHETTO, WHO WERE CONDEMNED TO ANNIHILATION, TOOK UP ARMS, THE HEROIC UPRISING LASTED TWENTY-SEVEN DAYS.

Waiting for their hunger rations. Only 300 calories per person a day were allowed in the Warsaw Ghetto, and thousands starved to death daily.

The Jews were forced to dig their own mass grave before the execution. Even children were shot at such mass executions.

To mop up resistance centers, the Nazis set apartment houses on fire and watched as the burning inhabitants of the Ghetto jumped to their fiery deaths.

SS men taking Jews from their hiding places during the Ghetto fighting.

ews are rounded up for deportation to concentration camps.

Upon arrival, men and women with children were separated.

few neighbors would come over and we would pray.

"And then we couldn't leave our town. The Germans didn't let you travel any more. But I did, on foot. I walked 27 kilometers to find other Jews. [About 16 miles.] The Germans didn't let you gather because they thought we might organize. They made a ghetto of every little town. And after that came hunger. Hunger and fear came as soon as the Germans arrived.

"And soon there was no more food. Our bodies began to swell from hunger. I would see people dying every day. They would drop dead in the streets. I saw my own cousin die from hunger. My mother died from hunger. I used to try to visit my mother. She wanted a little thing, like thread. I would tie the thread around me under my clothes. She would try to sell the thread. Oh, the Germans gave us ration cards to buy food at Jewish grocery stores. But they had shot the Jewish shopkeepers. The Jewish grocery stores, if they existed at all, had no food. So we smuggled and bought on the black market.

"But [strangely enough] some bakeries were allowed to stay open. They had a little flour to make bread. It's hard to explain how this was if you didn't live through it. You are permitted to starve slowly. Whoever could stand the starvation lived. Who ever couldn't, died.

"The Germans wanted their *Final Solution.* How does one go about achieving a final solution? We were still people. They tried to degrade us. In a town next to ours they, the Germans, chased out all the people. They came in the middle of the night and made them undress and chased them out into the streets, naked. They took the young men away to build dams for them. They made the young boys carry heavy stones with their hands. And many of the youngsters died because they could not carry the stones.

"At fifteen, ah the Germans believed, at fifteen years you didn't have a right to live any longer. From one day to fifteen years they had to be shot. My brother had a little boy, fourteen years. He was so smart. He came and said to my brother, 'Daddy, you see, you still have a chance to live. They are going to take you to camp and they are going to give you work. I have no chance to live.' He cried his heart out. He knew!"

The German occupation had now extended into 1941. Nacha married the boyfriend of her childhood. He was old enough to be allowed to live and young enough to dream. In the mathematics and logic of the German occupation they were allowed to live, to die slowly of starvation. There developed an innate resourcefulness that has no explanation, that perhaps arises from a will to live. For some unaccountable reason the ghetto, which the Germans had created where Nacha lived, was not complete. She continued: "We were able to contact people we knew before the war began. We'd smuggle in a cow or calf. And we'd take a few pounds of meat to Warsaw. They [the Jews] would grab whatever we would bring in. Everytime I went I'd think I was going to be captured and shot. I never thought I would be able to return again.

"I went to Warsaw before the ghetto was complete. It began slowly. The Germans would take things away slowly from the people, their money, their children, their food. After 1941 the town was closed. You couldn't travel, you couldn't smuggle.

"There were guards on the road. If the Poles caught you, they would bring you to the Germans to be shot. You had to fight the Poles and Germans. The Poles were sometimes just as bad as the Germans. In my town, however, there was one family hidden by a Polish family. They kept them because they had been given something of value. But in the end they shot them. And as the war came to an end they thought the Jews would be on top. They didn't know who would come first, the Americans or the Russians. So they shot all the Jews."

It was in September of 1938 at Munich that the Allies (Britain and France) gave Hitler virtual carte blanche to invade Czechoslovakia. Shortly thereafter, Hitler annexed the Sudetenland and Czechoslovakia.

On November 7, 1938 another giant step toward the liquidation of the Jews was taken. On that day a German Jewish 17-year-old youth named Herschel Grynszpan assassinated the third secretary of the German Embassy in Paris, Ernst vom Rath. The boy, whose father had been deported to Poland in a boxcar some months before, intended to kill the ambassador, Count Johannes von Welczeck. When Grynszpan showed up at the embassy Rath (a man who ironically despised the Nazi anti-Jewish policy) was sent to learn what he wanted. The Jewish refugee shot and mortally wounded him.

Within 48 hours of the assassination a wave of Nazi retaliation swept across Germany. On the evening of November 9th, Goebbels issued instructions that "spontaneous demonstrations" were to be organized and carried out through the night. The actual organizer, Storm Troop leader Reinhard Heydrich, coordinated the SS, police force and security service in a rampage that became a night of terror for German Jews. Heydrich ordered party and SS leaders to burn all synagogues (except those near German property) and destroy all Jewish apartments. As many Jews as necessary (especially wealthy ones) were to be sent to concentration camps after arrest.

Almost immediately after the order, as was reported in the *New York Times,* "...almost every town and city in the country" was affected. "Huge but mostly silent crowds looked on and the police confined themselves to...making wholesale arrests of Jews..."

While Jews attempted to flee their burning apartments, they were shot at by demonstrators and police. Within hours after Heydrich had ordered the demonstrations, at least 815 shops were destroyed, 171 dwellings set on fire or destroyed, over 100 synagogues burned, as many as forty killed, the first of six million—and twenty thousand arrested.

On November 10th, Propaganda Minister Goebbels issued the following statement; "The justified and understandable anger of the German people over the cowardly Jewish murder of a German diplomat in Paris found expression during last night..."

The burning, looting and violence continued all day. One American observer witnessed one Jew being dragged from a shop, beaten and chased by a crowd while a second Jew was dragged from the same shop by a single man who beat him as the crowd looked on.

In two days, store windows of Jewish shops were smashed in every city. Insurance claims for broken glass alone came to five million marks. If these claims were met, they'd bankrupt the companies.

Goering, who was angered by the massive insurance claims, reportedly told Heydrich, "I wish you had killed two hundred Jews instead of destroying so many valuables."

Three days after the *Kristallnacht*—"The Night of the

Broken Glass"—an infuriated Goering met with his staff and decided that as punishment for the murder of vom Rath, the Jews would pay for the destruction of their own property. "For their abominable crimes," as Goering put it. Insurance money was confiscated from all Jews and, in effect, given back to the insurance companies. "The swine won't commit another murder," he said.

It was time, the Nazis decided, to completely eliminate Jews from German economic life. But first, the Jews would be made to clean up the mess caused by the demonstrations. Goebbels and Goering decided the Jews should clear out burned down synagogues and build parking lots in their place. They insisted that Jews be completely excluded from all aspects of German life. On November 15th, Jewish children were barred from attending public schools. Later it was decided that all Jewish businesses and property would be turned over to Aryans. Jews would be compensated with bonds from which they could draw the interest but not the capital.

Mid- November of 1938 was the first time the German government had actually organized and carried out a vast program against the Jews. Total elimination of German Jewry was now official government policy. There could be no turning back.

World opinion rose sharply against Hitler, but he reacted with equal venom. Hitler believed the world was being usurped by Jews, and he was not about to let Germany go down with the "Jewish world conspiracy."

THREE

THE BEGINNING OF
THE FINAL SOLUTION

Kristallnacht, the Night of the Broken Glass, was to signal the beginning of the end for all German Jews. Within one month, on December 13, 1938, "Aryanization" became the law of the land. Jews were ordered to turn over all businesses, shops and industries to 'German' interests. The time had come, as one high-ranking German official stated with no suggestion of subtlety, "to kick the Jew out of Germany."

Three years earlier a concerted effort had been begun to remove from Germany the children, through the auspices of Youth Aliyah. "The Movement of Children" was ostensibly concerned with the emigration of youngsters from Germany and Austria to England to stay with private families who had agreed to care for them.

The condition of their right to emigrate was based on the fact that they would *not* go on to Palestine. To say that the Jews were unaware of what was happening in Germany years before *Kristallnacht* is to do a disservice to their sensitivity. Children were being accepted in the Scandinavian countries and the Netherlands as well. While considerable money was raised in the United States for their care and transport, the American government was, at the time, unwilling to admit them as refugees. When the war broke out children were still being sent to Denmark and Sweden. The ages of most of these children were between six and eighteen. For the most part, this included the age group the Germans deemed expendable. By August of 1939 the British consulate in Berlin had closed down, cutting off visa applications for the large crowds of children who had gathered outside.

In the early days of the evacuation of children from Germany (for that's what it really was), they were sent to Britain, and to the Netherlands. In the United Kingdom, many of them lived with families in the countryside in Kent and Scotland. A month before the war broke it became increasingly difficult to get ships to take the children.

The British Home Office had given permission for the children to come to England. But their eventual destination, a fact not recognized by His Majesty's Government, was that their final destination was Palestine.

Their entire 'training' program was one of indoctrination about their future lives in Palestine. The Youth Aliyah Schools were, for many of them, the only schooling they would get. You recall that, initially, Jews were to be driven from Germany. This explains why the authorities were allowing the children to leave. In fact it became imperative that those children, who had been decreed stateless, should be given first priorities. Countries which allowed the children to enter, France, Luxembourg, Belgium among them, insisted the children were to be considered in a state of transit. The officials of Youth Aliyah in Germany were in a position that was complicated by the situation in Germany, and they attempted to make some orderly procedure out of rules and regulations which were not only grotesque but not designed to serve the Jewish community—and at the same time fulfill the German predilection for orderliness. Exit visas and permits from the host countries had to be obtained. The children had to be gathered in one central point, coming from all over Germany to Berlin. This, in itself, was understandably a most complicated problem of logistics. Then, the British began putting quotas on the number of children they would allow into the country. How does one determine which child had to be left behind?

Up to the invasion of Poland the Germans had permitted the emigration of children, with a precise calculation that did not reckon with the British reluctance to accept them. Few German Jews, on the other hand, were permitted to attend the World Zionist Congress which was held in Geneva in the fall of that year.

In the beginning of 1939 Hermann Goering had issued a directive, designed to promote the rapid emigration of Jews from Germany. German citizens, in effect, were to be expelled from their own country.

This authority to permit Jews to leave was in complete

contradiction to Hitler's own words, which he said in a speech in the same month Goering's directive was announced: "We are going to destroy the Jews."

If German attitudes toward the Jews were outwardly ambivalent, this was consistent with Hitler's political alliances. Caught up in the first thrust of the war was the country of Poland. Squeezed between opposing forces of anti-Semitism were the Polish Jews. Adolf Hitler's primary goal that early spring of 1939 was the destruction of Poland. Despite the fact that Britain and France had signed a mutual defense pact with Poland in April of that year, Hitler moved against the Polish state. On September 1, 1939, World War II began with the German "blitzkrieg" (lightning war attack) on Poland. On September 3rd, Britain and France joined their Polish ally. The Soviet Union, which had signed a peace treaty with Germany, waited to occupy the eastern half of Poland after the German invasion was complete.

If the Ribbentrop/Molotov pact was designed to prevent Germany from fighting a two-front war it had precisely the opposite affect on the Jews of Poland. As Nacha had indicated, there was an obvious confusion in the minds of Soviet sympathizers in Poland. There was, however, no confusion as to the fate of the Jews. Warsaw was gutted by German bombers in a matter of hours after the war began.

In *Escape,* Bernard Lipman describes what it was like for a twelve year old, living in Warsaw, during the attack. He recalled:

"The entire Western horizon was covered with rapidly approaching planes...The planes came in small, little formations, some of them shaped like a 'V' and some of them shaped in straight lines...The planes were squat, ugly things with a long cockpit and one huge bomb hung underneath the fuselage. As I watched, the first plane began diving. As it came down faster and faster a whining noise began. At what seemed like the last minute the plane released the bomb and pulled away. I watched the bomb as it continued down towards a neighborhood a block or two away. There was an enormous explosion that rocked the foundation of our building. Smoke and debris shot up into the sky. It was all suddenly very real."

Hitler justified the rape of Poland by accusing that country of inciting war. "The Polish nation refused my efforts for a peaceful regulation of neighborly relations," he would tell the world.

Almost immediately after the occupation of Poland, Hitler imposed sweeping racial policies on the devastated nation. On November 23rd, 1939, Jews were required to wear a six-pointed star. A Jew caught without the star could be executed on the spot.

Anti-Jewish policies were many pronged. Shortly before the war broke out an anti-Jewish editorial had appeared in *L'Action Francaise* which suggested that the British with the help of the Jews were trying to drag France into the war. As William Shirer observed in *The Collapse of the Third Republic,* this was the very same theme being espoused in the controlled Nazi press in Germany. The French cabinet ministers who had been urging Daladier to be firm with the Germans were accused of coming under the influence of a 'Jewish clique in London.' The paper railed, "....If today our French people will allow themselves to be slaughtered unsuspectingly and vainly at the will of forces that are

English speaking Jews, or at the will of French slaves, then a French voice must be raised to proclaim the truth."

Anti-Jewish policy in Europe fed directly into Hitler's own Jewish plans. The Jews were caught between the Scylla of Hitler's overt anti-Jewish program and the Charybdis of latent anti-Semitism in the rest of the world. Five days after Hitler began the war against Poland, Cracow, the second largest city, fell. A few days later the Polish army was in complete disarray. In a week Russia would move in to pick up her share of the beaten country. Caught between them were the Jews.

Within a year, Jews were rounded up and isolated from the non-Jewish population in big-city ghettos; the largest was in Warsaw, where nearly 500,000 Jews were forced to live in a small section of town, literally sealed off by walls and German guards from the rest of the population.

Although there is no official, written document which foretells the Final Solution, the ghettoization of Polish Jews was the first step in the eventual annihilation of 6 million.

Occupation soldiers were told to make a distinction between the enemy. Non-Jewish prisoners of war, for example, were to be treated with dignity and respect. However, Jews were to be regarded as "poisonous parasites," and to be considered, not just the enemy of Germany, but "of all mankind."

Reinhard Heydrich was responsible for solving the Jewish Question in occupied Poland. Along with his "Einsatzgruppen," (mobile SS units assigned to combat the civilian enemy), Heydrich used mass murder, on-the-spot execution and torture to 'handle' Polish Jews.

With Adolf Eichmann present, Heydrich outlined his plan for Polish Jews. His *Einsatzgruppen* would concentrate Jews in city ghettos for eventual deportation. Jews would be transferred out of Germany and other occupied areas to Poland. Although Heydrich alluded to some sort of final plan for the Jews, it was never formally spelled out. However, during the following months when Jews were sent to labor and concentration camps, all activities were kept strictly secret.

From this point on all correspondence on the *Final Solution* was classified top secret (*geheime Reichssache*). Even special rules for the use of language (*Sprachregelung*) were used to prevent victims and the world from learning the truth about massacres and concentration camps.

Life in the Polish ghettos decayed rapidly. Money and food grew scarce. Jews were alloted half of what non-Jews were rationed. Outbreaks of infectious diseases, particularly typhus, became widespread.

In the beginning Jews were able to evade many of the regulations imposed on them. Some simply slipped off their armbands (with the Star of David) and went into town. Most Germans could not tell they were Jewish. Clandestine records were kept. Underground newspapers were published. But as Germany secured its hold on Poland and other nations, including the occupation of Denmark, France, Belgium, Holland, Norway, Yugoslavia and Greece between the years 1939 and 1941, life in the ghetto grew more torturous and barbaric.

★★★

Like all Jewish families, Bernard Lipman and his parents knew that when the SS knocked on the door, it was bad news. One evening, while he and his parents were visiting a friend, three SS men knocked on the door, then pushed it open. The SS men stormed into the house of his father's friend, Mr. Buterfas. They demanded to know where their son Zigmund was. Lipman continues his eye-witness account:

"Mr. Buterfas told the sergeant several times that Zigmund wasn't home. The sergeant refused to accept the answer and started to beat up Mr. Buterfas. The sergeant and another man punched him several times, then knocked him to the floor and kicked him. At this point their 18-year-old daughter tried to protect her father. The older soldier knocked her to the floor and told her to mind her own business.

"The beating and the constant demands for Zigmund went on for several minutes. The rest of us sat frozen in fear.

"At this point their baby started to cry. One of the soldiers looked briefly at the crib and then at Mrs. Buterfas. A look of real terror crossed her face and she started for the baby. Before she could take two steps the soldier ordered her to halt. As we all watched, horrified, the soldier picked the little baby up by its feet and, hefting it once, smashed its head against the ceiling.

"The baby went limp after the first blow and hung from the soldier's hands dripping blood. The SS man looked at the baby for a second as if analyzing it, smashed it against the ceiling again, and tossed it back to the crib.

" 'That's not the way to do it,' said the sergeant, matter of factly. Grabbing one leg in each hand the sergeant then proceeded to literally rip the baby apart. It made one of the most horrible sounds I have ever heard in my life.

"Mrs. Buterfas fainted. Mr. Buterfas went into hysterics. The rest of us were too stunned to move...Zigmund was rounded up and later transported. Mrs. Buterfas died a few days later from the shock."

***

By April, 1940 the Germans had given up on a plan to send all European Jews to the island of Madagascar, where they would be worked to death. Instead Hitler ordered the Polish ghettos to be sealed.

Various worldwide Jewish organizations (including the Palestine rescue committee Vaad Hatzala) with offices in many countries tried in vain to communicate with Jews inside the Reich's control. Unfortunately the Allied forces fighting Germany prevented communication with anyone inside occupied German territory. The mailing of food, clothing and other materials was considered aid to the enemy. Polish Jews and others under Nazi rule were totally isolated from the outside world. The Nazis accelerated their plan to exterminate the Jews inside their own territory. Jewish emigration was over.

European Jews faced another problem almost as bad as the Nazis. The Germans often rewarded those who pointed out Jews. Of course the punishment for harboring a Jew or even being suspected of helping one was met with severe and the ultimate punishment— death!

Many Baltic citizens were helpful to the Germans in pointing out Jews for extermination. Large crowds of Poles watched as Jews were beaten by German soldiers. For the most part their attitude was one of indifference towards Jewish citizens. The Danes, led by their king, would make an overt effort to help save Jews from Nazi terror.

The Jews were not immediately tortured and killed. Slowly and systematically, the Germans sapped their strength by literally starving them in the ghettos. Their ability to resist was weakened over a period of months. In smaller towns, the Germans came in without warning and, within days, quickly rounded up and killed hundreds of Jews, preventing any organized resistance.

Most civilized people simply could not believe the Germans really did what was suggested. By the time they saw their own children beaten and murdered it was too late.

The Nazis were expert at camouflaging their real intentions. As they herded Jews into cattle cars for the extermination camps, many still could not believe they were headed to their death.

Despite the fact that emigration was no longer possible, thousands of Jews fled Nazi rule any way they could. Thousands drifted on the high seas for months, hoping to be picked up by friendly ships. Their own ramshackle boats were more like floating tombs as many died of starvation or committed suicide on board.

In June, 1940, France surrendered to Nazi Germany. Hitler stood at the English Channel, ready to conquer Britain and later Russia. In fact, one year later, Hitler ordered his forces to invade the Soviet Union. He also took one more step towards the genocide of the Jews. On March 1, 1941 Hitler directed Himmler to go to the German concentration camp at Auschwitz and order Rudolf Ness, the camp commander, to expand accommodations to 100,000 prisoners of war. It was understood that the area for the new prisoners of war would be mainly for "political" enemies rather than captured soldiers. These political enemies included mostly Jews and Russian Bolsheviks. So much for "Non-Aggression" pacts.

★★★

Shortly after the occupation of Poland, hundreds of so-called labor camps were constructed. Shortly after his fourteenth birthday Bernard Lipman was picked up and sent to Lublin. As Lipman recalled, "My luck ran out in March of 1940."

Rounded up near his home along with hundreds of other Jews, he was marched seven miles to a suburban train station. "By the time we reached the station I had become filled with a deep sense of unreality."

At the train station, Lipman was herded into a cattle car with hundreds of other people. The trip took about one day and by the time they arrived all the people were already half lifeless.

At the concentration camp, Lipman worked on a platform near a river where he shoveled mud and sand. The work was exhausting, and at night everyone sank to sleep, weary, lonely and wondering when and if it would ever end.

The Germans kept enlarging the camp, sending in more and more prisoners as the weeks went by. As time went on camp life became increasingly more dangerous, as Germans would sometimes kill prisoners on a whim. Lipman remembered one incident which depicts the early horror of these camps:

"The Feast of Passover came while I was at this camp. This is a very important religious event for Jewish people. One of the rules of Passover calls for the eating only of unleavened bread.

"On the day of Passover I found myself working alongside two very religious brothers, Moses and Jacob; one nineteen, the other twenty-three.

"In the middle of the morning, Moses suddenly collapsed from exhaustion. Rushing over, the SS guard said, 'What are you lazy Jews up to now?' As I helped the other man lift up his brother, he said, 'Today we are only allowed to eat matzoh, sir, as it is a religious holiday.' "

At this point the Germans tried to force the two brothers to eat bread. When they wouldn't comply they were beaten senseless by the guards. "I watched this last scene from the catwalk," said Lipman. "Watching the rifle butts thud into Moses' head I fainted and fell into the river."

With both brothers too injured to walk, Lipman and several others were called out in the middle of the night to bury them while they were *still alive*. Taken out in the middle of the night Lipman and the others were forced to dig a large grave. Suddenly, Jacob turned and tried to run away. Three soldiers raised their rifles and fired. Lipman and another man were ordered to drag Jacob, who was still alive, back to the grave. Jacob "was sweating profusely and in a great deal of pain," remembers Lipman. "Blood dripped from him as we picked him up by the arms and legs."

The Germans ordered Lipman and the others to throw Jacob in the grave. With rifles pointed at their head, they lowered Jacob into the large pit. Meanwhile Moses, who was still throughout, pleaded for his life. "Sooner or later you have to die," said one of the Germans. "It might as well be now." With that he pointed his rifle at Moses' foot and fired. As Moses fell in agony, one of the soldiers pushed him into the grave with his brother.

"The leader then turned to us and ordered us to fill the hole. None of us moved for a moment. Then several rifles were cocked and slowly we picked up the shovels and began to throw the dirt down on top of Moses and Jacob. Moses struggled to a sitting position and began to cry out, first to the Germans and to us, and then later as the dirt began to rise about his body, to his mother.

"It took almost half an hour to bury him alive. Near the end I began to get sick and all of us began to shovel at a frantic pace to stop that terrible voice calling to his mother out of the pit."

Bernard Lipman was lucky. Within several weeks, he escaped from the camp under the cover of darkness.

★★★

As Hitler turned his attention towards the Russian front his zeal to eliminate Eastern European Jews (whom he blamed for inciting Russian anti-Nazi policy) increased. Heydrich's special military *Einsatzgruppen* was increased in size. These political soldiers were trained to do one thing; kill Jews along the eastern front. They received their indoctrination from Himmler who instructed this so-called elite corps that the "Jew-Bolshevik" was the mortal enemy of the German people and the German state.

As Hitler's armed forces overran the western part of Soviet territory, the *Einsatzgruppen* would enter a town and quickly begin its work. Jews were called out for the purposes of resettlement. After handing over all their valuables, they were ordered to remove all their outer clothing. They were then marched to a large ditch, forced to their hands and knees, and shot to death. The corpses were then thrown into the ditch.

The map of Europe in June of 1941 had changed radically since 1933, when Hitler came to power. Jews in Austria, Czechoslovakia, Poland, Denmark, Norway, Luxembourg, Netherlands, Belgium, France, Hungary, Rumania, Bulgaria, Yugoslavia, Greece and parts of Soviet Russia, were being exterminated by the men of the Third Reich.

In July of 1941, Himmler, the chief transmitter of Hitler's will, let it be known that the time had come to hasten *The Final Solution* to the Jewish problem. Hitler also transmitted his order for the extermination of the Jews to Goering, who in turn put Heydrich in charge of the actual operation. On July 31, 1941, Goering sent Heydrich the following orders, to the effect that rather than eliminate Jews through emigration, as earlier policy dictated, it was now time to work for a *total solution* to the problem of all Jews living in German territory. This was the first direct order to kill all of Europe's Jews.

As early as January, 1941, Hitler had indirectly let the world know his intentions. In a *New York Times* story dated January 31, 1941, Hitler talked of his statement of 1939 when he suggested that, if international Jewry pushed the world into a war, it would be wiped out. Hitler said the European war would now show that he was right in 1939.

"Already," Herr Hitler asserted, "our racial views are gripping people after people, and I hope that also those people who are today our enemies will one day recognize their internal enemy and that they will enter into a front with us—the front against international Jewish exploitation and corruption of peoples."

By the time *The Final Solution* settled over Europe in the summer of 1941, thousands of Jews had already been ruthlessly murdered by the Germans.

★★★

For tens of thousands the war came to an end with horrifying suddenness. For many tens of thousand more the horror was just beginning. Men and women who had lived and reasoned together, had survived petty arguments and enjoyed mutual pleasures were tormented by individual drives for survival. One woman could be inwardly satisfied that it was not her husband or son who was either summarily shot or shipped to a *no exit* concentration camp. They did not think of themselves as part of the Holocaust. That was a cover term the civilized world was yet to apply to the years of torture and torment, of sadistic pleasure and murder, of mad 'scientific' experiments on prisoners, of perversion gone rampant, of the kind of orgasmic satisfaction that came with the slaughter of the innocent.

Nacha endured the German occupation. But how did the child who was to suddenly become an emotional adult bear up? How does the adult remember? She remembers with a shudder and a gush of words and a pause to recall the torment and then she does so with words which are not always lexically satisfying, but have a meaning so intense that to change them does an injustice to the feeling which prompted them.

Nacha continued: "We lived in this little town, with hunger and fear, with sicknesses, with lice being thrown on our heads. With airplanes they would cover the whole town with lice. And if we went outside in the evening (after curfew) they shot you right and left."

Then a sigh, then a recall of another step, "And then it was time to go to the concentration camps."

But there would first be days of unrelieved anxiety.

In the way that the oppressed have to communicate, by signs, by codes, by a word unspoken, by a nod or raised eyebrow Nacha learned of the fall of the surrounding communities. She received letters—[How were they written and by whose direction?]—that she shouldn't worry. "Here comes a letter, 'Don't worry, they take us to camps. We have working camps. We're treated pretty good.'

"They made the Jews write those letters from the trains that were taking them to the camps. If one escaped those trains and came back to the city he would tell you, 'Remember, we are going to Sabine (sic) and it's extermination.' So then here comes a letter, 'Don't listen to all these people. If you see someone running away, don't pay attention to him. We are in camps. We are treated well. We're having work.' "

And the months and years are condensed by words into paragraphs, into moments of retelling. But it was now the beginning of 1942. "When they started the real extermination. We were so degraded. They could come in and tell you to take off your clothes." The camps lay ahead when to take off one's clothes and shower was preparatory to the gas chambers.

"I remember, we would sell shoes which my husband had made, wooden shoes. We would sell them to the Poles. We thought maybe the Communist would save us. We still didn't believe that total extermination was going on around us. One man, I think he was a member of the Communist party, would say, 'It's impossible. It's never

The concentration camps were surrounded by wires through
which passed a high-voltage current.

Day in, day out, new transports of prisoners crammed into cattle wagons, came to the extermination camps from various parts of occupied Europe.

The treachery and cruelty of the SS men were without limit.
Prisoners were forced to play while they accompanied their
comrades to the gas chambers. Musicians were kept alive for
this very purpose.

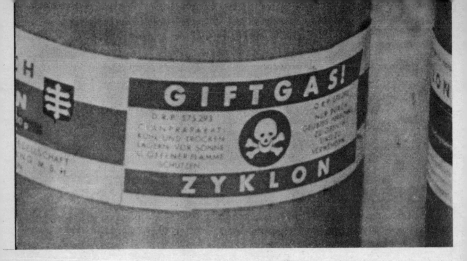

The infamous "Zyklon B" gas was used in air-tight chambers to suffocate millions of people. The bodies were then piled up and burned in crematorium ovens.

Loading bodies into the furnaces for cremation.

At Treblinka extermination camp, mothers carrying children on their way to the gas chamber.

The founders of the concentration camps — Himmler, Kaltenbrunner and others — inspecting the Mauthausen camp.

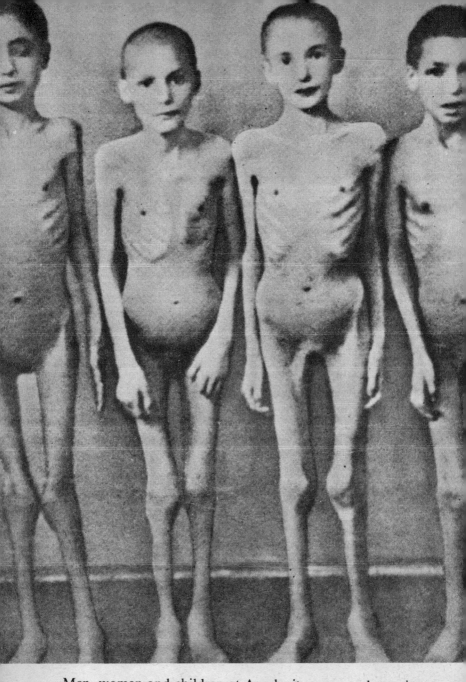

Men, women and children at Auschwitz were used as guinea pigs in criminal "scientific" experiments.

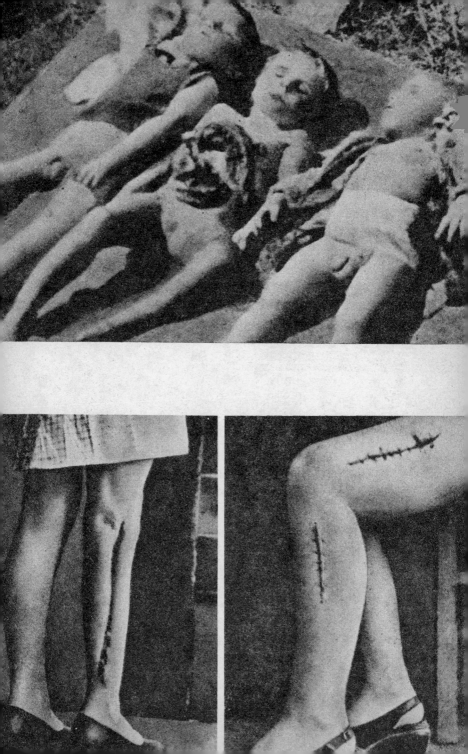

Roll calls were a form of torture at Mauthausen. Some lasted eighteen hours without a break. Here, boys between 12 and 15 years old, forced to line up.

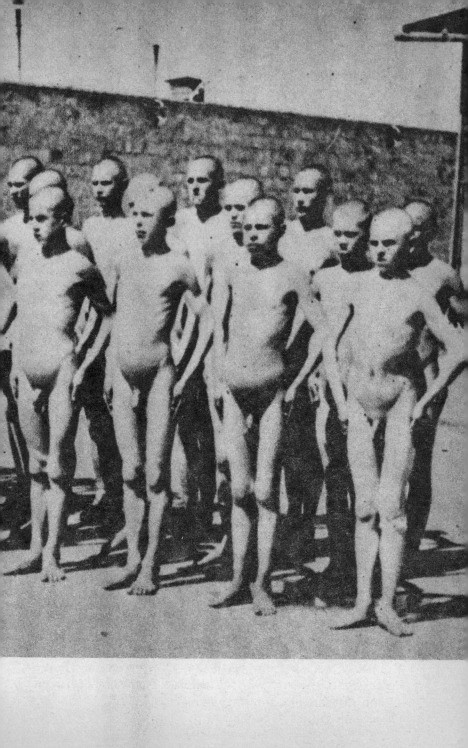

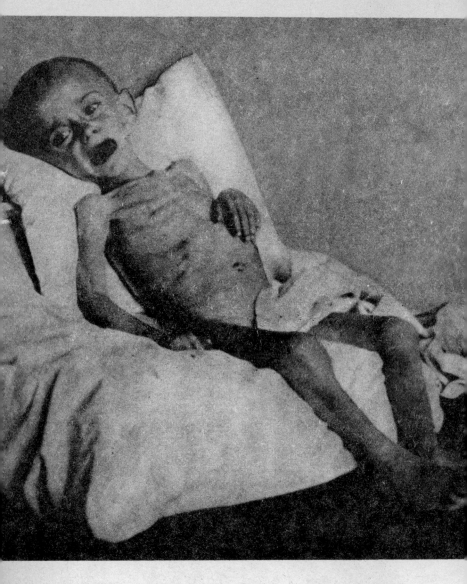

Tiny victims of a monstrous madness — at Auschwitz.

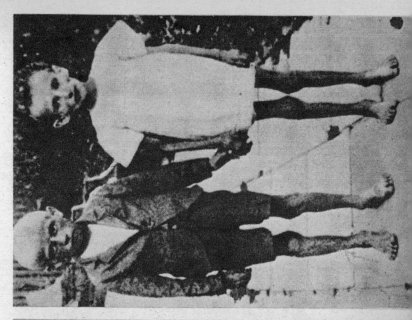

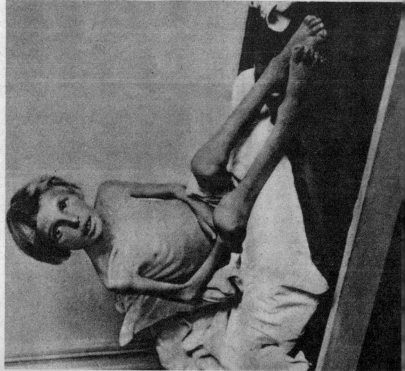

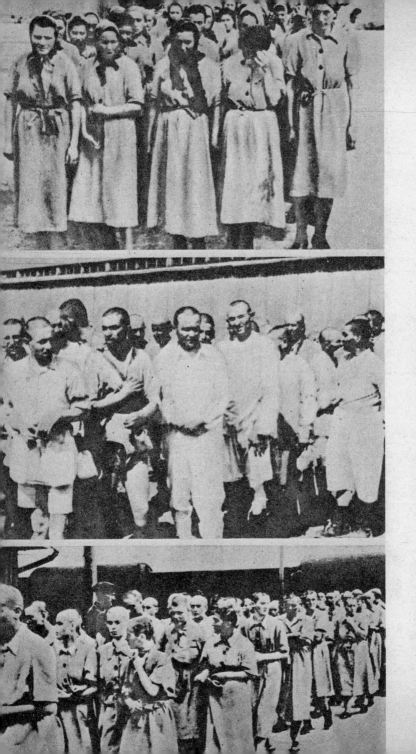

Dehumanized living at Mauthausen...and the dead at Auschwitz.

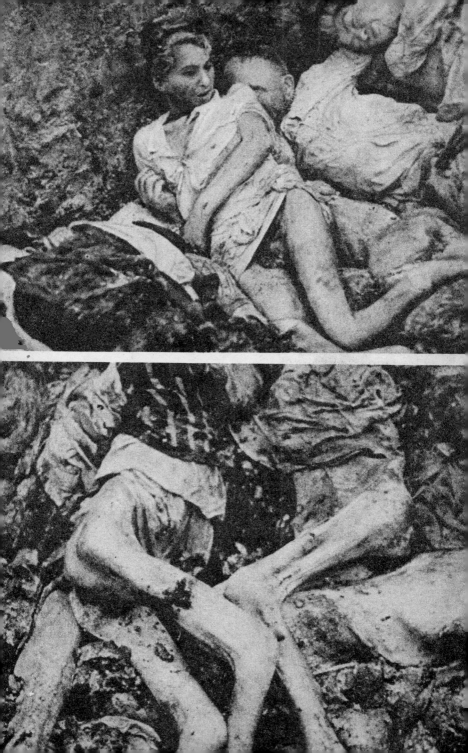

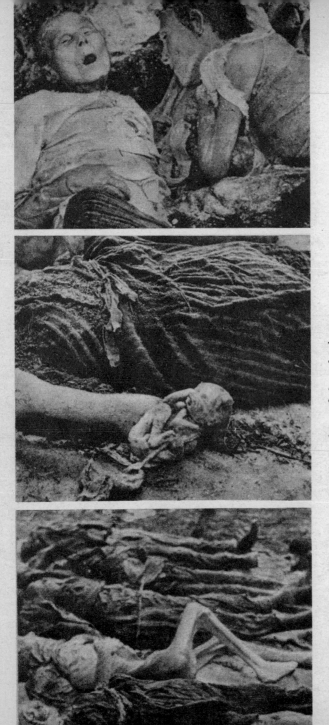

January 1945. Just before the liberation of Auschwitz.

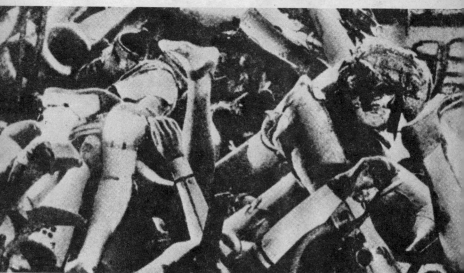

All that was left of millions of human beings...glasses, combs, tons of hair, shoes, artificial limbs.

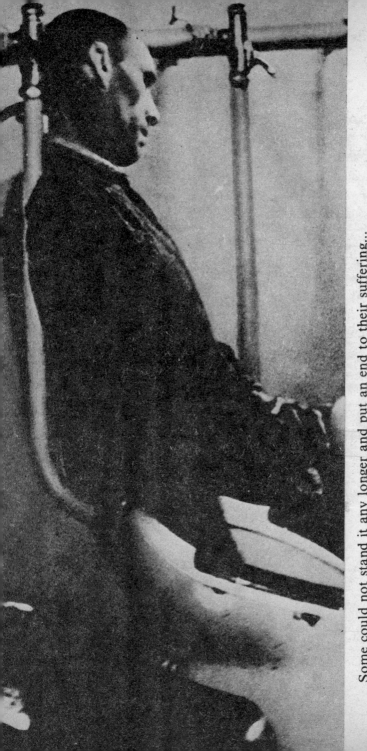

Some could not stand it any longer and put an end to their suffering...

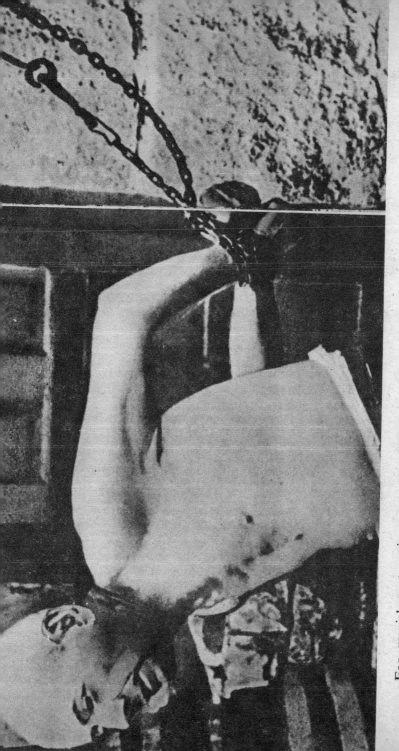

For punishment, prisoners were often thrown into 3' x 3' dungeons, and chained to the walls.

...others tried to escape — in vain.

going to happen. I assure you, it's just plain fate. It's just propaganda. Nobody can let them do systematic extermination'."

Is the explanation of why so many Jews went to the camps without a struggle, why so many lined up and did as they were told before being executed, that they simply could not accept the truth of *The Final Solution?* Who would believe the fact of total extermination, of the implementation of the *Final Solution?* And who were they who tried to mitigate the rumors, deny the magnitude of what was truly happening? Agents, spies, dupes?

But the facts of Nacha's townspeople being taken away, of the slow disintegration of neighboring towns was too much to hide, too much to deny the fact that was happening.

And Nacha remembered the end of her town. It was two days before "the liquidation of the city." She tells it haltingly. "This most pious of men with a long grey beard; he was praying on the balcony. And we were terrified at what this man was doing in plain sight. There was no more work, no more life in us. We were all like dead bodies, but alive, like shadows. We knew the Germans were coming. And this man says we should all get kerosene and burn ourselves tomorrow before they come. And you know, the Lithuanians were the real murderers. I came in contact more with Lithuanians than with Germans."

And they didn't burn themselves because there is a hope to live, a hope that the frightful end will not be the end at all. And when the Germans came to cleanse the town of its Jewish inhabitants, Nacha hid.

"They took all the people to the wagons (sic). Not only

did you go in trains with sixty or a hundred or two hundred people, you stood packed air tight. You couldn't lie down. You couldn't sit down. The bastards had cleaned out the cars with a chlorine solution, which would burn your eyes out."

Nacha, with her husband and her sister and with others who numbered twenty-four, went into hiding in a cellar bunker that had been built to hold eight. Outside, the liquidation of the city had begun. The words pour from Nacha's mouth, little bothered by grammar or editorial niceties or structured sequiturs. They are words of remembering, of nightmares and never forgetting. With just some small editing, a punctuation here and there, they become real, not synthesized by a research writer, not polished by a sub-editor, not made to fit a predisposed pattern by a proofreader.

This is how Nacha remembers, thirty-five years later. "This is the end of the liquidation of the city. Some people have their own bunkers. They would take in other people, whomever they can. Some people push themselves in, too. They would know that this man had a little cellar. So whoever could, pushed themselves in. My aunt was left out. She found a baker who was living in a bunker. He had lived with her and he took her in. We had enough water for week. How long was it going to be? Whoever will save themselves will come out and live again.

"We had bricks which would cover up the opening, which was about four feet high. When you put the bricks back in place, from the inside, you would never know there was an opening. We had six small children and they would always be crying their heads off. We could hear it getting quieter on the outside and we knew they (always *they*) had taken the people away. Two days went by. We could hear the Poles come back to take what belongings, what possessions the Jews had left behind. They were ordered to clean the town and bury what dead were there. If they didn't obey the Germans they were shot on the spot. The Lithuanians did their job better than the Germans. In their black uniforms, they would do the job. When it was a little quiet we would go out of the bunker. One goes out to get some barley. There was nothing else to eat. One would say, 'It's quiet on the street.' [Quiet is for the dead!] One lady's two children were crying with hunger. She goes out with her two children, her husband and her brother. They never come back. I don't know what happened to them. We are all getting sick in the bunker. There is vomit, body waste. It is becoming unbearable. We hear the Germans coming back with their dogs. The Germans knock on the walls of the buildings. They come to the third basement, the second basement, then our basement—and they knock on the wall. [Apparently the bunkers in which Nacha and the others hid were built on tiers, camouflaged to resemble a solid surface.] The dogs don't stop barking at our wall. We are finished! A father holds his kid's mouth shut so he wouldn't cry. But the Germans go away. The father and his son leaves with his son. Another family takes their two children out. [They will not wait to be caught. The tension has increased to the point where one must move out to live, even if doing so means capture and death. Such is the contradiction brought on by fear.] We wait another day. We hear the wagons come to pick up the dead. The soldiers have shot whomever they see come out of the bunkers. A paper is forced through our opening. It read: 'Go out from the bunker because there's no way you are going to save yourselves. Everyone else who was in bunkers are out now.' They take all the Jews who come out of the bunkers. *They* are Poles. They group us together. When we come out the Poles are there, with the police and the fire department. They wanted everything we had on us, what possessions we had left. The Poles take us away so we won't be shot by the Germans. Some of us who had jewlery hidden give it to the Poles. I didn't have anything. There are others who had come out of different bunkers. For a day and a night we are kept in one spot. And then some of us are selected to go to a nearby town where there is a munitions factory. They need people who can work. I was young and strong. I could work."

FOUR

THE NAKED, THE DEAD
AND THE LIVING

Nacha's story continues:

Nacha's memory of the Holocaust burns strong within her. She remembers, as do most of us trying to recall traumatic events, not necessarily in chronological order, but in order of importance. What may seem slight now, loomed important then for her, and remains equally strong today. For a moment she went back in memory to the old, bearded religious man who was praying on his balcony. She saw him through a crack in the brick wall that encased her hiding place in the cellar bunker. She remembers the German soldiers coming up behind him and taking him away, down into the house, then out into the street. She doesn't recall whether he struggled. But he knew they would come for him. She saw him disappear, out of her sight. She heard his voice reciting, "Sh'mah, Yisroel..." (Hear O Israel...). And then there was a shot. She knew he was dead.

There are remembrances of small acts and grotesque results. There was a woman, in her sixties, Nacha recalls, who went to the owner of the house in which they were hiding. The woman offered the few possessions she had if they could be hidden longer. She was buying time, not life. The old woman returned, stripped of her outer clothing, the jewlery ripped off her fingers, her body beaten. There was no time to be bought.

The memories of the camps Nacha was taken to merge into one blur of shooting and screams and death. She remembers hearing the sick cry out in the hospitals, then shot to make room for the new sick, who would, in turn, be killed to make room for the dying. There are memories of putting on performances for the other girls her age. They prayed during the holy days.

She was at Belsen where there were no blankets, no heat to ward off the unbelievable, killing cold which lasted more than five months. Work projects began as early as three in the morning. There would be a body count at 5:30. If any were missing, random selection of those present would be made—and they would be executed. The prisoners organized themselves, so that if someone was missing—too sick, most likely, to join a lineup—others would shuffle from line to line so the Germans would get their accurate count.

There are tales of dead prisoners being propped up in line in order for Germans to get a correct body count. It didn't seem to matter whether the bodies were alive or not, as long as the numbers were correct.

And what was it like, on the way to the camps, and in them? Nacha continued: "The Germans came out with their whips. On the end of each was a big piece of iron, to hit you with. We had to walk 20 kilometers, without stopping. There was one woman who was pregnant. She gave birth to the baby along the way. But she continued without the child. There were a lot of children with us on that walk. There were children without their fathers and mothers. There were babies sitting on the streets crying. Everybody was afraid to pick up the babies.

"Only the older people picked up the babies because they knew they were going to die anyway. I saw mothers leave their children with their parents. We saw thousands coming out of the camps. They were skeletons. They would ask us, beg us, 'Do you have a piece of bread?' But the Germans wouldn't let you give any to them even if you had food.

"The Germans shot the ones who couldn't walk any more. As we neared the camp we had to step over dead bodies. I knew some of these people. They had come from my town.

"In the camp the starvation started—and the shooting. We stood in line. A German named Botinslager (sic) took out three girls, three beautiful girls, seventeen years old. I knew one. Her name was Kata. He took them to his headquarters. He used them and later he shot them.

"In the camp we lived like pigs; lice was on the straw. One big (room) for a thousand people. In the morning we have to go to work. We have to dress up and be pretty. You have to scratch but you don't dare, one is fearful what delousing means.

"In the factory, every Friday, a German lady looks at you and your hair. If you have lice she cuts your hair off. She shaves your head.

"Every other night Botinslager needs women. He picks out a few girls to bring to his headquarters. We see their bodies in the garbage. We are afraid that any one of us might be next.

"Sometimes they have too many people from one town. They take out the ones who aren't so good looking or look pale. They take out twenty, fifty, 100. They take them into the woods and shoot them.

"It is 1942 and I will be in this camp for two years. There was no place to run. The Poles wouldn't accept you. They would line us up and shoot every tenth person. You pray you won't be the tenth.

"If the Germans want to teach us a lesson they take the people who tried to run away and make us watch them get shot. I would close my eyes.

"If the Germans had just a suspicion that you had some contraband (we used to smuggle in thread to sew or something to wash with), if they found a piece of thread they would shoot you. Children under fourteen were shot."

A sigh, a rest, a pause. What about the sick and the hospital?

"If you got sick the Germans would take you to the hospital, which was a stable. Every Sunday was their day to have fun. They would shoot out the hospital."

Nacha is quiet. It is difficult but she goes on.

"One German officer wanted to see how people made sex in the street. He takes a young boy and a young girl from my camp and puts them on a bench and shoots them as they make sex. This was considered a privileged camp.

"Another officer wanted some boys to catch a live mouse. The boys would catch the mouse and bring it to him—and that is why they were not shot."

And about her work.

"I worked on a machine that made very small (sic) bullets. There were Jews who tried to smuggle out bullets for the partisans. They were hung. The Germans made a spectacle of the hanging. I learned how to adjust the machines so the Polish foreman could go home and he would leave me in charge. I had a better chance to live because I had more work to do. Once the guards wanted to take me but the Pole wouldn't let them.

"I was taken to another camp (Chanterhall?). I guess they were afraid the Russians were getting too close. We lived in what was like a small ghetto. There were still people in their homes and they tried to help us. What did the Germans do? They shot everyone and brought us the boots and shoes and dresses and coats. They told us they would give us what we wanted. But if we went to get them ourselves they would shoot us. I never went. I made myself invisible.

"My husband was in another camp. He worked in a chemical factory. The Poles beat him to take his clothing. He used to come to me sometimes when they let him. He was yellow from the beatings. He was a singer and the Germans would like to hear him sing, so they would give him soup. He would have been able to live because the Germans liked to hear him. But his Polish foreman beat him to death.

"In the beginning of the war they didn't let him work. He had food because they wanted to hear him sing. When he came to see me later he looked like an old man. He said to me, 'Nacha, I'm going. They've registered me to go. If you live through this, name your first born after me.' There was much love."

It became important to Nacha to remember the separation from her husband and from her family. It preceded her confinement in camp. But in memory it came later.

"My sister was registered to go. The Germans came in the middle of the night and yelled 'Heraus.' A brother would want to go in place of brother. I wanted to replace a brother. They wouldn't let me.

"We couldn't kill ourselves even if we wanted to. We have to wait to let them do it. When we heard about the assassination attempt on Hitler we thought they would kill us.

[This would put the time somewhere in July, 1944. On the 21st of that month Hitler broadcast to the German people that a bomb had been placed in his room by Col. Graf von Stauffenberg. One member of Hitler's staff had been killed. *Der Fuehrer* broadcast, "What fate would have been in store for Germany had this attempt on my life succeeded, is too horrible to think of."]

"The Russians were getting closer so they took us out of the factory. We saw soldiers on horseback fighting Russians in airplanes. We thought we could be saved. We called, 'Open the doors, open the doors.'

"They took us to Buchenwald (?). We go on trains. We are on the trains maybe three days and three nights and we have a little bread. The train stops and they take out all the men. There are electrified wires around the train. I saw a lot of people go to the wires and kill themselves. We arrive at Burgenbenser, a death camp. As we are going in, a German prisoner of war, a Russian lady, tells us, 'You are going in here. You are going to be treated as people. We are prisoners of war. You are going to go into the showers and you are going to be cleaned.'

"The Germans took us from the train into the showers. We said, 'We're going to be gassed'. There are no showers, we were all naked. But there was really water. They gave us soap. There was written on the soap R I F,

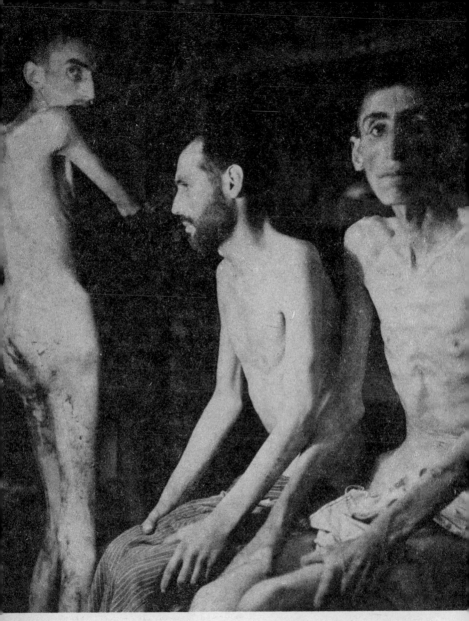

When the U.S. 80th Division took Buchenwald they found these Russian, Polish and Dutch slave laborers who had lost nearly 100 pounds each in their eleven months of imprisonment.

One of 150 political prisoners burned to death by Nazi SS troops at Cardelegen, Germany, as he attempted to escape.

Prison laborers at Camp Flossenberg, near Weiden, Germany, emptying crematory furnace of bones of slave labor victims. The bodies were disposed of by the Nazis after they were killed by phenol injection, machine gunning and hanging.

Political prisoners at the Belsen concentration camp were starved and tortured, the dying and the dead buried in a common grave. When the Allied soldiers arrived they found the air so foul that birds avoided flying overhead.

Death becomes commonplace and the prisoners themselves are emotionally drained of pity as a victim is carted to the incinerator.

The living at Buchenwald. — The dead at Buchenwald.

Bodies on the way to the crematorium.

Survivors at Wobbelin concentration camp on the way to medical care after liberation.

the German initials for the words *Clear*

as soap made from the Jews who were burned at Auschwitz. They took the hair from the women and they made mattresses. They took out the teeth and looked for gold. In my husband's camp was a young man who wouldn't give up any of his possessions. They found some coins in his pocket. The stuffed *shit* in his mouth until his stomach burst.

"After the shower they say we are going to get shoes and clothes. Our hair gets frozen. We get clothes. A big lady gets a small dress and a small lady gets a big dress. We were laughing and crying at the same time.

"We are taken into the barracks and we lay down close together to keep warm. I was to stay in that camp maybe four or five weeks. Sometimes we would go forty-eight hours without food. Our work was to carry iron, iron beds, and iron pieces of furniture. We carry the iron, maybe a half mile or a mile. They make us do this just to make us work. The German army is already finished. But they still have time to do this. By now it is February, 1945.

"They count us every morning. When we were liberated we were so skinny. Anne Frank was in that camp. She couldn't make it. She was in another part the same time I was there. There were girls from all over Europe. We would register ourselves to be shot. We didn't want to die slowly. We would be bombarded by Allied planes. We are put on a train that doesn't move for seven days. A German tells a young girl he is a doctor and gives her bread so she will stay with him.

"But the girls were good. We would give our life not to sleep with a Nazi. If they gave me a piece of bread I wouldn't sleep with them.

"If a Jew had a piece of bread he couldn't get a girl. If he did she wouldn't be looked on so good. But later when we thought about it, maybe we should have.

"Finally the train is fixed and we go to a camp called Bulgow (sic). There are German women running the camp. They gave us bread and coffee. I don't remember if we did anything. We went into the barracks and just sat there. They, the Germans, came in every day for inspection. We had no food. We were starving. They took us out from time to time to work. I don't even remember what we did, if we did anything. The Germans wanted the barracks to be clean. They would come in every day for inspection. They wanted to kill us. But they didn't want to leave any evidence.

"Also, the young German soldiers didn't want to go back to the front. They wanted to be busy with us in the camps. In March they took us to another camp. They would march us by a restaurant and we grab potato skins from the garbage. They would shoot whomever they would see doing this and would tell us the person was going to get poisoned.

"Once we had to clean out a basement and there were some potatoes there. My girl friend, Tibel, and I found the potatoes. We put a number of them in the linings of our coats. We didn't know whether we would be searched. In one of the camps I was in we were searched every day. The guards had found some food on some of the inmates and beat them. After the beating the watch was changed and my girl friend and I were somehow not searched. We brought the potatoes into the barracks and hid them under the straw. The SS would come in. A woman would search and see to it that everything is clean and immaculate. She touches the straw but doesn't find the potatoes.

"By this time the Germans, it seemed, were trying to appease us. They were afraid the Americans would come any moment. So now they gave us potatoes, the first since I was taken away from home. It became a little easier. They marched us out of camp again, to another. The Americans are coming closer. They know the end is near and don't know what to do with us.

"There are rumors that we are going to be taken to this city or that we will be killed. They take us to a camp outside Dachau. At night our barracks are strafed with machine gun fire. It is the German youth who are doing the killing now. There is no more German army. However, I must tell you it was a death march to Dachau. Everyone who got tired along the way was shot. We carried a girl friend so she would not get shot.

"In this camp there were Polish prisoners. The men thought we would be nice to them. But there was fighting all around. There were mortar shells exploding in the streets. Prisoners and Germans were killed.

"On the 29th of April the Americans came in. Now I really wanted to cry. There were potatoes. There was food. But the American soldiers had to go on.

"The SS women wanted to show how good they had made the camp. They told the Americans to go over to the girls, us, and ask, what did these women do to you. We were still afraid to say anything. In fact one woman said, 'Oh, the Americans are here now. But I bet you the Germans are going to come back.'

"I was afraid, then sad. The war was still going on. The soldiers didn't let us out right away. Maybe the Americans thought we would harm the Germans. But the Jews don't know how to kill. The Russians came and killed the Germans, everyone they could find. They even burned them alive until they were stopped by the Americans and the English. The Russians told the Jews to go out and kill whomever they wanted.

"Then I realized I was alone. I had no more family. I was alone.

"The Americans sprayed the camp with DDT. They gave us what food they had. They didn't have too much. So we had to eat pork. I was kosher. When the Americans found us we were in bad shape. After two weeks they took us to a Displaced Persons camp. But we were still afraid of the Germans. We were afraid when they asked us to take showers. We were put fifty-four girls in one room, two to a bed. The camp was still run by Germans, including the doctor and the nurses. We would ask ourselves, 'What the hell are the German men doing here?'

"It would be more than another month before we would be truly liberated. I remember, after the war, seeing a German baby and thinking I would kill it. But I didn't, of course. But I remember the tanks that ran over the people in my town. I could still hear women calling out from their graves, 'I'm still alive, I'm still alive.' I remember the moans and the groans and the dead.

"The war was over, but we were hostile. We were broken. Some women said they would never marry Jews. After the war, when my daughter was born she looked unreal to me. It is only lately that I see how Jewish children should live. I used to see children as chickens, who would soon be killed.

"I am stronger now than I ever was. The war hardens you. I used to live where the subway was deep (in New York City) and a bomb could not reach down there. We can hide our children and ourselves."

Nacha Katz lives with her second husband and family, remembers the Holocaust. They have their own business. The times are different. Yet it was not long ago she lived ready to escape from a war which would come to America. The war has not come. But the memories of the Holocaust will not fade either.

FIVE

HOPE AND NO HOPE
AND HOPE AGAIN

Menachem Warshawski and his wife Sharon live
in one of New York City's outer boroughs. Some time
ago Sharon deposited with the Yivo Institute in New
York City a remembrance her husband had set down.
After the war he found himself in Israel, caught up in
another war, this one to help preserve the State of Israel.
Wounded, he was hospitalized. There was a time for
recollection, for wonder, for trying to understand what
had happened to him during the Holocaust and what it
had done to his spirit.

What follows in this story, as he wrote it, with the same
appreciation of his orthodoxy. (God's name must never
be spelled out.) To tamper with what he wrote is to
suggest that one who has not been there knows better.
This is his perception of a time of his life. It is his

perception of reality—and that is the truth.

The words were written in Israel in June, 1948. One war and one Holocaust had barely ended. Another war had begun.

My back hurts. I am in a cast. It is very hot here. They took the only fan to the other ward where they brought in seriously wounded soldiers today. I am in an Israeli army hospital. I am 18 years old.

Four nights ago I was carrying a back-pack of 50 kg. of TNT to blow up a wadi overpass on which the Arab army and vehicles moved. When the shooting started, I jumped and hurt my back. We did blow up the overpass, but I had to be assisted back to camp.

Now the heat intensifies the smell of medicine, iodine and disinfectants. The ones who can are writing letters to their families. I can't—there is no mail being delivered to the Auschwitz crematorium. But I write anyway. It is just a belated "Thank you" note.

It happened three-and-a-half years ago. It must have been in the beginning of November or thereabouts. The year was 1944. I was fourteen years old then, which was not too young to be a slave prisoner in a German concentration camp. My residence was Labor Camp Gleivitz IV, a branch of Concentration Camp Auschwitz. My number was B-6816. I was here for being a Jew. I had no sentence to serve. I became resigned to the idea of remaining here until the very end. "End" meant to be the end of the war with the Germans defeated. But mainly it meant my end, in the gas chamber or its like.

Air alarms were heard then quite often. I could see the countless bombers, day after day. The feeling was that the war was coming to an end. Somehow it didn't seem to matter anymore. When I began a day in the morning, I was never sure that I'd see the evening. The daily perils made even the near future look like no future at all. People were dying here daily from starvation, torture, bullets or from lack of hope. By then there was only a slim chance that any of us would live to see the end of the war.

This day was exactly as any other day, except for the first bitter and freezing cold weather. On the way to work I could see and feel the winter coming at us with its cruelty and destruction. Hands and feet began cracking open from frostbite. The frost cracked open a previous injury on my foot but somehow it didn't seem to cause any pain. My senses were too numb to notice such a minor discomfort.

Our clothing was limited to a light prison jacket and trousers, a shirt and shorts. I was extremely lucky to own a cotton sweater. It was given to me by a Hungarian doctor the day he extracted my infected tooth with an instrument he made from a spoon. But the sweater didn't do much to stop the merciless cold wind which was blowing continuously at us. I tried to convince myself that it was only a matter of time, that I must and will get used to the cold, that I will overcome it eventually. But deep inside me I was very doubtful about whether I would see the spring sun again.

It was still dark when we arrived at the road which we were constructing. The German foreman divided us into small working gangs. The "Capo" beat up one of us even before we began to work. He needed to impress some of our many superiors with how easily he could handle us.

We were issued a pick for each man and a shovel for each two men. My partner on the shovel was a man named David who, in the barrack, occupied the bunk below mine. He was very respected by the men who happened to know him. He often had a good word when it was most needed. He was a religious man. I often saw him praying at work, at camp, or when marching.

I was using the shovel when I saw David cry. I was tempted to ask him why he was crying, but I couldn't think of anything to say to make him feel better. The oddest thing about it was that very few of us had any tears left to cry with. David, noticing the look in my eyes, said, "I hope G-d cares more for my family than he cares for me."

I too began thinking of my family that was separated from me the day we were sent by camp. If only I could let them know that I am alive. If only... If only... If only...

For several moments the cold didn't bother me anymore. I was far away from all the hell around me. I was beyond the reach of the "SS." Many memories flashed through my young mind. I could clearly see mother lighting the Shabbat candles with all the family around her. I could see father blessing my younger brother and me on the eve of Yom Kippur. I could see the beautifully set seder table with all the relatives around it right in front of my eyes. I was home, I was free, everyone was there; it felt warm and good.

Suddenly my thoughts were interrupted by David's warning whisper, "The Capo." For an instant I wondered if I wasn't dead already—sent by G-d to hell—and that this was what Gehenem was all about. Feeling an icy wind between my shoulder blades brought me back to reality. With the dry eyes of a veteran sufferer I looked up to heaven and barely murmured, "Why, oh G-d... Why?"

I had seen some of the prisoners put on empty cement bags underneath their shirts to stop the wind. I too was very tempted, but also very afraid. The lightest punishment for such a crime was ten lashes held in the middle of the camp square, where many died before being able to feel the tenth lash. I knew that for me it would mean certain death if I was caught. But later, when the wind increased in strength, I too put one on.

Some men were told to put up a fence from old construction lumber for the "SS" guards, the German foreman, and the "Capo" to shield them from the wind. When I looked back a while later, I saw the "SS" man standing close to a roaring bonfire. It hurt too much to look at it.

A man working beside us fainted and fell to the ground. We tried to revive him before being noticed, but we couldn't help him. One of the "SS" guards came over with the "Capo." The "SS" man kicked the fainted man several times. The man opened his eyes long enough to say, "Shoot!" pointing a finger to his own head. The "SS" guard said, "It would be a waste of a bullet. You will die anyway."

I heard a slight click; the safety catch on the "SS" guard's gun was released now. The "Capo" made us return to work. One shot was fired. When I looked over my shoulder, I could see the gun barrel only inches away from the man's head. Two men were ordered to pull the dead but still warm body aside. Then I could see the "SS" man and the "Capo" laughing on their way to the fence and the burning wood.

Although it was not the first time we witnessed the murder of a sick or weak prisoner, our spirits were sinking lower and lower. Not a single word was spoken, for each of us could see himself collapse for the last time, which seemed to be not far off at all.

After a long silence, a man who was working in front of

us spoke up. *"I will be better off dead."* By the way he said it, I knew he meant it. He looked very bad. His skin was tight on his face, as if it was the only thing that kept his bones from falling apart. His eyes looked as if they were about to fall out of their sockets. His face had no trace of hope or faith. I knew what was coming next. I had seen it happen too many times. (Please, oh G-d, help him!)

For a while, this man kept on repeating the same sentence over and over, convincing himself into his own death. Then he walked over to the bonfire where the guards were standing. He took off his cap and stood at attention, the procedure before speaking to one of them. When asked what he wanted, he said that he wanted to be shot. His answer came with a rifle butt in his face and some kicks when he fell down. I helped the man return to our assigned work.

(continued on Page 169)

After rescue, one prisoner, who had survived the holocaust, mistakenly believes he has been forgotten. Now, over thirty years later there are some who have forgotten.

Over 4,000 Russians and Poles were kept prisoner at Wobbelin. But the death rate was in excess of 150 per day.

Corpses at Lager-Nordhausen concentration camp left unburied by the retreating Nazis. Bodies of slave laborers were found in humanly unrecognizable states. The dead lay beside the sick and the dying; filth and excrement covered the floors. The Nazis made no attempt to help the sick or alleviate the pain.

Crippled Russian and Polish prisoners rescued by Allied troops from Mauthasen concentration camp.

One of eleven camps at Landsberg where Jews were imprisoned. The average prisoner, if able, survived five years as a slave laborer.

This, too, was once a man.

Two officers of the 94th Division count the bodies of Gestapo victims who were shot and buried near Landwehr, Germany.

One of his eyes was injured. Most of the blood was congealing on his face before it reached his jacket. The moment David saw him, he began applying snow to the beaten man's face, trying to encourage him, to convince him to hang on to life just a bit longer, explaining that it is a matter of weeks, perhaps even days. David's words no longer had any meaning to him. He was just standing and shivering without even being aware of his physical state.

We knew that this man was dead even though he was still standing. We knew that nobody can live here for long without a will for survival. This man lost his hope, and hope was our only weapon to fight back with, and all that kept us alive. Even a false or an imaginary hope was better than no hope at all.

When I saw the same guard who shot the man who had fainted earlier in the day coming towards me, it was as if the Angel of Death himself was approaching. He told the beaten man to run across the field if he wanted to be shot. The beaten man wanted to run but could barely walk. He was limping very badly in the first few steps of his final walk. The man stopped, waiting to be shot. He was shouted at to go faster and farther. After a few more steps, a bullet pierced the cold air. The man fell wounded. He had gotten up only halfway when another shot was heard. A third shot was fired direcly into the man's head from above him.

As the "SS" guard walked past me, I could clearly see the broad, sadistic smile on his face. The rest of the guards were standing around the fire and laughing about his poor marksmanship. David murmured a quick Kaddish. I found myself saying "Amen" without moving my lips or my clenched teeth. The constant why...why... why...continuously reverberated in my mind. Why do we have to be lowered to such depths before perishing?

Few among us seemed to be disturbed. The soup kettles which had not yet arrived were more bothersome than the cold-blooded murders which had just taken two lives from among us. We were living for the minute. Later, tonight, tomorrow or any time, any one of us might be dead. We were aware of our lot, but we were cold and hungry now.

An "SS" officer arrived just before dark for his routine check. The word spread that there will be no soup. We had suspected as much. The "Capo" read the tattooed numbers on the dead men's forearms while an officer marked them down in his report book. Before returning to camp, the "Capo" ordered me and three more men to bring the two corpses back to camp. Two of us went to the man who was shot last.

He was covered with snow, his body frozen, his face expressionless, the same as it had been before dying. We checked his clothing for something that could be useful for the living. He had nothing extra. His shoes were worn worse than ours. I had a deep guilty feeling for wearing the extra sweater and the cement bag.

His last words about being better off dead were still ringing in my ears. Now I wasn't sure who was better off, he or I. Suddenly I wanted to cry out for father. I wanted him so much. I wanted to be a child again. But to the Germans being a Jew was the same "crime" for young and old.

After being counted—the dead and the living—we put the corpses into the "dead ditch" which held up to fifty corpses. We did receive our soup, and we were counted again before the light went out. Although the barracks weren't heated we had no trouble falling asleep.

When the morning bell rang, we had only a few minutes to make our bunks to geometric perfection, clean the barracks and get out to the camp square. There we waited for an hour or two before being counted and led to work.

Having left the bright light around the electrified fence behind me, I looked at the sky with its bright stars. I wondered how long it had been since I picked a lucky star for my own as a boy. Now they were no longer shining for me the way they used to. Even their twinkle irritated me. They too were laughing at us, the way the "SS" guard did after each murder.

What kind of G-d is there in those heavens above, planting millions of Hitlers on earth to tear us to shreds and millions of stars above our heads to ridicule and laugh at us? Wasn't there any truth to what my parents and teachers told me about men and G-d? What was the real truth? Only that every man, like every wild animal, is by himself and for himself on this earth? Some day G-d, when I will stand before You, I will want some answers.

That day I was late, very late with my morning prayer. I had no more use for it. When the soup arrived at noon, I wasn't even hungry or bothered by the sharp frost. Watching the men line up in a hurry, I wondered if the gamble for the small chance of living through this hell was worth all the suffering. I could see myself drifting and slipping down the "dead ditch," having no strength to hang on to the edge.

Standing last in line with my tin can in hand, I wondered if there really had been Maccabees or soldiers of Bar Kochba, or if they were myths to brighten the days of darkness of our people. If then, why not now? Was there a better time for it than now? Or are we worse than the "dor hamidbar," we who let ourselves be slaughtered, and worse yet, let ourselves be degraded to a low, lower than any insect? Aren't we capable or worthy of saving the honor of our people anymore?

Do you, too, G-d treat us with the same indignation as the Germans do? Perhaps you are right because you too saw the two men, your children, who wanted to be shot yesterday. And I too found justification for their deeds yesterday.

Please, oh G-d, let me be a Maccabee or a Bar Kochba soldier. But if you think I am not worthy of it anymore, let my ashes fertilize the ground for a new proud life for my people. But until that time, let me...let me... Truthfully, I have no demands left. My eyes are dry of tears, my heart is empty of feelings. All I was taught to do was to pray, and that, I can't do anymore, except to repeat that childish wish to be a Maccabee or a Bar Kochba soldier. Please don't take this wish away from me.

Now, here at the military hospital, I turn my head to the soldier lying next to me in order to tell him: "Thank you for having let me see the title of your book. It meant a lot to me." "What? 'The Maccabees'?," he asked with astonishment. "You can read it if you want to. It is boring, though." "No, thank you. I know them very well."

Turning my head the other way I thanked G-d for the tear in my eye, for it was the first tear since long, long ago.

SIX

ON TO THE FINAL SOLUTION

"I am filled with hatred and anger at what they have done. I cannot forgive. I cannot forget. There's no way."

Bernard Klein; Auschwitz survivor interviewed by NBC TV News; May 4, 1978.

> *...And death in the camps*
> | | |
> |---|---:|
> | *Auschwitz* | *2,000,000* |
> | *Belzec* | *600,000* |
> | *Chelmno* | *340,000* |
> | *Majdanek* | *1,380,000* |
> | *Sobibor* | *250,000* |
> | *Treblinka* | *800,000* |
>
> *TOTAL 5,370,000*

Long before Hitler began using the large extermination camps for the annihilation of the Jews, he began systematically 'liquidating' deficient Germans; that is, those Germans who were mentally or physically incapacitated. In *Mein Kampf* Hitler spelled out his notion of euthanasia for the benefit of the Aryan race. Hitler asserted that those who were deformed, visibly sick or who had inherited a disease that could be passed on should be declared "unfit for propagation."

By the spring of 1939 Hitler had already put to death thousands of mentally retarded and physically deficient children under an umbrella organization called *The Reich Committee for Scientific Research of Hereditary and Severe Constitutional Diseases.* The organization, of course, never made public its real function.

In September of 1939 Hitler officially ordered his chief medical officer in charge of the euthanasia program to destroy all persons judged incurably sick. While most children slated for death were killed with injections, adults were sent to one of six laboratories where they became the victims of Hitler's first program for mass murder.

Most of the adult patients were gassed with either carbon monoxide or a cyanide gas known as Zyklon B., the gas used at the major German concentration camps later in the war. Eventually the German public began to realize what Hitler was doing to the German indigents. Shortly after the first gas installation was set up at Brandenburg in 1939, citizens could not help but notice the thick black clouds of smoke belching out from the cement chambers. People used to refer to the vans which carried the sick to these gas chambers as "murder boxes."

Eventually some members of German society began to

protest the mass execution of so-called racially valueless citizens. In 1941 Hitler reluctantly stalled his program. Still, he managed to send nearly 100,000 German citizens to their premature death.

When Hitler called on Himmler in the summer of 1941 to implement the Final Solution of the Jewish Question, precedent for mass killing had already been set. It was simply a matter of incorporating the idea of euthanasia for racially unfit people on a larger scale. In the summer of 1941, Himmler told the Einsatzkommandos that orders to liquidate the Jews came from the top and that they bore no personal responsibility for their actions.

In the summer of 1941 Himmler told Hoess (the commander at Auschwitz) to enlarge the camp. Because of its easy rail access, isolation from populated areas and physical surroundings, it had been picked as the first camp for mass extermination of the Jews.

Late in the summer of 1941 Eichmann came to Auschwitz to discuss with Hoess methods of liquidating the Jews. Among other techniques, Eichmann recommended gassing prisoners with carbon monoxide while showering, as was done with mental patients in Germany.

Since Hitler had already successfully eliminated thousands with gas, there was no need for further experimenting. Jews were to be killed with gas!

The summer of 1941 marked the first construction of the Vernichtungslager—the annihilation camps. Civilians, proficient in the use of Zyklon B., were sent to Auschwitz to instruct the staff in its use. By September, 1941, Auschwitz was operational. Its first victims were several hundred Russian prisoners of war and Jews captured by Heydrich's Einsatzkommandos. It was a success.

Other death camps went under construction and were rapidly completed. Chelmno in Poland was the first major camp to be finished. Its intended victims were Jews from the Lodz ghetto. In the winter of 1941 Belzec was completed. Majdanek, near Lublin and Treblinka, some 50 miles from Warsaw, was also completed in a short time.

During the beginning months of operation, camp commanders couldn't decide on the precise method of extermination. Carbon monoxide gas was used at first, but after Rudolf Hoess (who was to be found guilty of murder) set up Auschwitz, he settled on Zyklon B. A crystallized prussic acid dropped into the death chamber from a tiny opening, the acid took from three to fifteen minutes to kill everyone in the air-tight cell. Auschwitz accommodated more Jews per gas chamber than any of the camps. While Treblinka could fit only 200 people in each of their ten chambers, the Auschwitz cells could accommodate up to 2000 at one time.

In the summer of 1941, Jews from all over Europe were being readied for the camps. Only Jews over the age of 65 and those who had fought for Germany in World War I were to be exempt from immediate extermination. These Jews were mostly confined at Theresienstadt, a camp which eventually became a 'model' camp; the only one which the Germans allowed foreign visitors to inspect. Aside from older people, the camp also housed very prominent Jews whose disappearance would be embarrassing for the Germans to explain. Unfortunately, most prisoners at this camp eventually found their way to Auschwitz, where they were killed.

After the order for the *Final Solution* was given, the SS was charged with responsibility for rounding up Jews from all over Europe. Jews were deported by duplicity as well as force. Often they were simply told that they had to be "resettled for work in the East." Usually they were allowed to bring their personal belongings with them, to insure the German intention that they wouldn't be killed. In the Polish ghettos, where thousands starved, the Germans offered bread as an inducement to take the train to resettlement locations. Eventually however, all Jews came to understand that resettlement was merely a euphemism for transportation to the gas chambers.

In March of 1942 the first major party of Jews (from Czechoslovakia) was sent to Auschwitz. The selection process to determine which Jews would die right away and which ones would work at the camps for the war effort was made at the railway station or at the camp itself. SS doctors had the prisoners form two lines, one for work, the other for extermination. Virtually all children under age 12 were marked for death because of their inability to do heavy labor.

At camps like Treblinka, Jews could immediately identify the death chambers. There was no pretense in hiding the finality of their fate. Auschwitz was a different story. There, the Germans attempted to fool their victims, although it wasn't easy. Most knew why they were there.

Told they were going to showers for delousing, prisoners were marched towards the gas chambers which were always well painted and had beautiful front lawns with rich flower beds. Over the entrances were signs reading, "BATHS." The inmates were encouraged to sing light, cheery songs as they entered the chambers. Then they were given towels and told to remove their clothes for the showers.

Upon entering the huge chambers, most prisoners (if they didn't know earlier) saw their real fate. As many as 2000 were jammed inside, making it virtually impossible to move, let alone bathe. Then the doors were slammed shut and sealed air tight. Orderlies stood ready to drop the Zyklon B. crystals through vents which led into the chambers. After pouring them through the vents, they were sealed shut.

The Germans watched 2000 people die through heavy duty glass portholes. The prisoners looked for water from the showers, but soon realized what they were getting was gas leaking from the vents. There was panic. Many rushed for the large doors, clawing and crawling over one another. Their anguish and pleas for help could be heard throughout the surrounding area. The Germans knew everyone was dead when the screeching subsided.

After approximately half an hour, the poisonous air was pumped out and the doors were opened. Jewish inmate corpse handlers (called sonderkommandos) were sent in under SS guard. They were promised their life for performing their function. Stepping through vomit, and the filth expelled from the mouth and bladder of the dead, they searched for valuables, removed teeth containing gold, and cut off the prisoners' hair, which was valued by the Germans for the war effort. They loaded the bodies into carts and dragged them across the yard towards the crematoria, where they were shoveled into open-hearth furnaces. Flesh blistered, blood and body liquid hissed in the burning flames. A dirty, black cloud of greasy smoke poured out of the chimneys. They waited for the bodies to completely burn, then raked the ashes out of the ovens and hosed them down in preparation for more. The entire process of transforming

2000 people into human ash took approximately five hours.

After several weeks of duty, the sonderkommandos were killed and a new batch was formed. The SS did not want witnesses talking about their methods of cremation.

From the summer of 1941 until the last days of 1944, Jews from all over Europe were transported to German concentration camps where most of them were immediately liquidated. As the war in Europe progressed Hitler continued to give the *Final Solution* priority over every aspect of the war. When the need for railroads, for example, to send Jews to their death competed with military use, Hitler ordered the military to find a way. He did not want to slow down the process of the *Final Solution*. Even when the Germans began retreating from countries such as Greece late in the war, they took railroad cars filled with Jews with them.

Towards the end of the war some exceptions regarding the transporation of Jews to the gas chambers were made. In occupied territories where there existed a high percentage of Jewish skilled labor, the army was told it could keep these Jews for the war effort. But it was rarely without a fight from the Gestapo, who had orders to take every Jew they could.

Hitler had a difficult time accepting the need to keep Jewish labor for the Reich. In the summer of 1942 he ordered that the 300,000 Jews (out of 1 million total workers) be released from their jobs and sent to concentration camps. The army was extremely hostile to this attitude, urging the Fuhrer to consider Germany's need for war materials. But the *Final Solution* was a policy of ideology, not rationality. Himmler issued a statement saying steps would be taken against all those who intervened in the so-called interests of the German war industry to help Jewish business. The army capitulated to Nazi ideology shortly thereafter. Aryans were to replace Jews who were employed by the Wehrmacht immediately.

Near the end of the war, the army had turned some of the Polish ghettos into labor camps for war production. However, the SS, under Himmler's orders in 1944, was ordered to completely evacuate Jews from Poland. So fanatical was the German desire to rid Europe of Jews *as soon as possible,* they would not listen to the army plea for Jewish labor. As the allies invaded Normandy in June, the Germans were busily deporting the last seventy thousand Jews from the Lodz ghetto to Auschwitz.

In many of the camps, among them Auschwitz, Birkenau, Ravensbruck, and Dachau, something like 10 percent of the Jews was kept on to work permanently (so long as they did not become too ill to work) for the Germans. Eventually, they were all slated for extermination. In fact, if those not chosen for immediate extermination were able to mentally and physically hold up, plus significantly aid the camp via their labor, they stood a good chance of living. These were the camp survivors.

From the moment they stepped aboard the trains which transported them to the camps, their lives were radically changed. Nearly 100 people were crowded in boxcars for the long rides across Europe to the concentration camps. The cars were torturously hot. There was no food, no latrines. People used to cleanliness were housed in cars filled with the stench of vomit, urine and excrement. By the time they arrived at the camps, the dehumanization process had begun.

At Auschwitz, where sixty thousand permanent inmates were housed, prisoners deboarding cars not slated for immediate extermination were immediately assaulted by German soldiers with whips, and dogs tearing at their feet. Families were torn apart, as they were herded into crowded buildings where everything, including their hair, was taken away from them. The mere size of Auschwitz was staggering: forty square miles, guarded by 5000 Germans.

Half-starved, sick and frightened into submission, prisoners witnessed indiscriminate beatings and murders. They saw men, women and children collapsed against electrified barbed-wire fences. They saw black smoke billowing above the crematoria, and smelled the stench of human flesh. They looked at corpses strewn along the road; some shot to death, others dead from starvation. It was all much too incomprehensible to absorb. These prisoners had already been subjected to the first phase of camp life: the disintegration of their ability to rationally understand what was happening to them. Some fell to the ground in despair. Others were taken away for interrogation, which usually involved great physical punishment. Others managed to continue to survive.

It has been said that those prisoners who lived past the first few days of camp life stood a decent chance for prolonged survival. The death rate among prisoners the first few days was high for a variety of reasons, some having little to do with actual physical punishment.

No prisoner, no human being could in any way have been mentally prepared to understand what camp life would be like. The horror of Nazi extermination camps was unspeakable as well as unthinkable. Many prisoners simply lost the will to cling to life after experiencing the first few hours of camp life. Others died of grief, knowing their families had been wiped out, their friends killed. Caught in a whirlpool of German atrocity, knowing there would be no escape, many prisoners saw little value living this kind of existence. Death for them was preferable to living.

Dasha Rittenberg, a survivor of several Nazi prison camps, recently told the *New York Times* what it was like to see death as a real alternative to prison camp life. Taken from her home in Poland at the age of 13, she spent much of her time at the Blechhammer camp, which housed mostly French and Belgian Jews. "I was covered with lice," she remembers. "I had boils the size of apples. I was bitten by dogs. I tried to hang myself...It's terrible to have survived. A tiger, a lion would not have survived."

As she watched the 1978 television program "Holocaust," (which portrayed the life of Jews in Nazi-occupied Europe and Germany) Dasha Rittenberg remembered her own camp life. When the television show depicted Nazi concentration camp life she said, "I couldn't wait to see them dead already, because they'd stop suffering."

Despite the ruthlessness of camp life, many prisoners did indeed choose to survive. When prisoners arrived, they were divided into several categories; political prisoners, inferior races (Jews and gypsies), criminals, and homosexuals. Each group wore a badge to distinguish its particular category. Jews were required to wear a yellow star of David.

As soon as they were off the trains, prisoners who were slated to live were stripped of all their belongings and given in return a set of clothing which included a white striped shirt. They also received a spoon, bowl and cup. Prisoners were then assigned living quarters; usually a space in the tiers of long rows of wooden bunks, overcrowded to as much as four times capacity. They were then assigned a work detail.

During the war, a large number of prisoners were employed by private industry. They were a plentiful source of free labor. A large proportion of camp prisoners were employed by the Reich itself, usually working on munitions. The average life span of a camp prisoner rarely went beyond nine months; most dying from a combination of disease and hunger.

From the first day prisoners were subjected to constant filth. There were few latrines in most camps. And the latrines which existed were an abomination. Typhus was common among large segments of camp inmates. Among its symptoms was painful and constant diarrhea. The stench was ever present. As prisoners lay in their barracks, it would drip over the bodies of those below, mixing with excrement left there from the day before.

Not only did prisoners suffer from other common diseases such as dysentery (which also produced prodigious diarrhea), they were subject to excrement harrassment by the Germans at any time. In fact, this was a common form of punishment meted out by camp guards. Sometimes guards would prevent an inmate from relieving himself; forcing him to stand or kneel till he virtually exploded. At that point he would be beaten and forced to grovel in his own waste. On other occasions, SS troops would sneak up behind a prisoner while he was at the latrine, then push him into the large pit. Many actually suffocated to death that way. There was no limit to this form of human degradation.

Sleep and food, basic needs of life, were commodities not easily attained at prison camps. Camp diets were at starvation level. Hunger was constant. The terrible need for food reduced the will to live and even drove some prisoners to cannibalism. Watery soup and minute portions of bread were the daily diet. The penalty for stealing food was death.

Sleep was also kept to a minimum. Daily, prisoners worked in a virtual state of numbness. The temptation to fall out from work and go to sleep was constant. It was, in fact, the only means of temporary escape from the insanity of prison life. The penalty for prisoners caught asleep was also death.

Aside from fear of starvation, possible deportment to the gas chamber at any time, prisoners also lived with the knowledge that they might be sent to German labs to serve as human guinea pigs for so-called medical research.

During the early part of the war Viktor Brack was appointed by Hitler to find a quick method for sterilizing Jews. Tested at Auschwitz, the Brack system consisted of irradiation of the reproductive organs of men and women. Another system tested out at that same prison camp was headed by a man named Karl Clauberg. He sterilized women by injecting them with a substance that burned out the womb.

At Dachau, experiments conducted for the air force involved subjecting prisoners to very high pressure and freezing conditions.

Other gruesome experiments were also performed. Hundreds of prisoners had bones amputated, muscles cut and organs removed. Those that didn't die remained crippled for life.

Those prisoners who ultimately survived the concentration camps found their survival rested on a combination of reasons, not the least of which was luck.

After an initial collapse into despair, some prisoners found a renewed will to live through caring for other prisoners. Sometimes a failed suicide 'shocked' prisoners into realizing the gravity of death. Whatever reasons prisoners used to continue living, they were complex and difficult to comprehend within the boundaries of human understanding. Oddly enough, the notion of 'hope' became irrelevant in terms of survival. There was no hope at concentration camps.

Learning to survive within the camp administrative structure was one method of assuring some chance for survival. Usually an appointed 'camp elder' was charged with maintaining prison order. Each block of prisoners had a foreman, who in turn was assisted by other prisoners. These prison appointees (mostly non-Jews who were often hardened criminals) were responsible to the *Kapos,* camp supervisors who in turn were directly responsible to the SS.

The SS rewarded cruelty, respected sadism. Many camp foremen were as ruthless and sadistic as the SS. But some were not. Still, they had to be adept in making the SS *think* they were. Thus, pleasing the SS was a crucial aspect of prison behavior. Sometimes through bribery, sometimes because the foreman became friendly with prisoners, he learned to behave viciously towards prisoners when the SS were around, but when they were away, he slackened off.

Very slowly, camps developed various sub-culture activities among prisoners. For example, some were able to hide prisoners singled out for extermination. Others were able to secure medicine by forging various requisition forms.

In time some prisoners found the will to resist within the prison camp. It took years in most camps to develop consistent lines of underground resistance. Most leaders were already political prisoners; some having lived in the camps from as early as 1933.

Most resistance was organized to foster better treatment from the Kapos. Prisoners might select a particularly harsh foreman, sneak up on him at night, and dump him in one of the open pit latrines. This was a direct message to other prison foreman that unless their treatment of prisoners improved, they would be next.

As the war progressed, it became apparent to some prisoners that the Germans were not doing well. In order to boost camp morale, prison undergrounds made sure they spread every possible bit of news around the camp regarding the defeat of the Germans. Some were even able to construct small radios and at night they listened to Allied broadcasts.

The underground also attempted to keep accurate records of daily camp activities, so upon the conclusion of the war they could share prison camp life with the world.

More than hope, it was the job of all survivors to somehow 'cheat' death, to find a way 'not' to die that day. As one ex-camp prisoner said after her release, "I thought of myself first, second and third." That is not to say there were no acts of compassion or selflessness among prisoners. But the reality of camp life and survival forced prisoners to deal strictly with their own survival rather than respond to emotions such as self-pity and remorse.

Those prisoners who stayed alive throughout their

prison internment managed to find some order in their existence. After their period of initial surrender to conditions beyond their control and understanding, they somehow were able to integrate their own lives with the chaos of camp life.

Towards the end of the war, with the Allies advancing on all fronts, the Germans found that they were unable to evacuate the remaining prisoners from the camps by rail. So they organized forced marches from camps in occupied territory. Mostly through starvation, these marches cost the lives of nearly a quarter-million Jews. Still there were Jews left in other extermination camps. And as Germany crumbled, the SS left the camps in the wake of liberating forces.

Out of the millions of camp prisoners killed (including at least 5 million Jews) only some 500,000 concentration camp survivors remained alive. All were mentally and physically broken; survivors of the worst holocaust in the modern world.

SEVEN

548 DAYS

"For killing vermin, lice, rats, etc..."

How does one describe a bridge to a child who has never seen a river? How does one describe the warmth of the sun to one who has been always blind? Menachem Warshawski asked how one can speak to children who may only think of the time of the Holocaust as a kind of docu-drama? He lived through it and is sometimes silent in the face of innocent questioners. But the information about those times needs telling and retelling.

One can still travel to Auschwitz and read the warning signs on the barbed wire fences. The cell blocks where the inmates were kept are still there. The guard houses and the gas chambers are now silent reminders of the Holocaust. The rooms where the victims' possessions, the gold from their teeth, the hair from their heads, were piled are still there.

Jews and non-Jews were slaughtered at Auschwitz and at nearby Birkenau. It is estimated that men, women and children from over twenty-eight countries were among the murdered.

In the United States and in Europe there are museums of the Holocaust. There are men and women of all faiths who are determined that the world will not forget, not because they want to live in the past, rather because they want to assure a more peaceful future.

There are Christians who know how their faith suffered, of the murder of the twelve Sisters of the Congregation of the Holy Family of Nazareth. During the Nazi occupation of Nowogrodek in northern Poland, they attempted to help those who were arrested. In turn they were arrested and, on August 1, 1943, were shot by the Germans and buried in a common grave.

It was a little more than a year later that a concerted effort was made to get the stories of Nazi atrocities to the outside world. The infant child young Bernard Lipman had seen battered and literally torn apart by German soldiers was a horror beyond belief. The continuous stories of children and adults buried alive, of wanton torture and the most obscene demands one human could make on another were yet to reach a disbelieving outside world.

In 1944 a Jewish office was set up in Britain with a major program for getting this information out. Documentations of Nazi atrocities were being recorded from those few who were able to escape the ever engulfing Holocaust.

The Jewish Central Information Office checked the survivors' reports as carefully as possible. What one individual went through, tens of thousands endured and died. Those who managed to escape did so by a combination of luck, intelligence, some outside help and even by a German obedience to orders (where the dead could be counted as 'live' bodies).

This is the story of Mordecai Lichtenstein, told in May 1945, after eighteen months in the Auschwitz concentration—or extermination—camp. He was born in Bendszin, Poland in May, 1912. A wood merchant by occupation he attended the Jewish Grammar School until 1922. He left his home town that year, to return in 1939 to be near his mother when the war broke out. He spoke German, Russian, Hebrew, Yiddish and, of course, Polish. His story follows:

Bendzin had about 30,000 Jews and 3-4,000 Poles that September, 1939. One of the first measures of the German occupation force, which consisted of Gestapo and police only, was to burn the big synagogue, the Beth Hamidrash (House of Learning) and the houses adjoining the synagogue. This was done by a special commando, the so-called "Brand-Commando," which used incendiary grenades. People who tried to escape from the adjoining houses were shot. The Jews were confined to certain streets which they were forbidden to leave. Anyone breaking the regulations was ruthlessly dealt with, or having even the smallest quantity of provisions not allotted by the ration scheme, had to report to the police. That meant "Aussiedlung" (deportation), the implications of which we did not grasp at the beginning. We only thought that these people were sent to labor camps in the East of Poland. The first mass deportation of about 2,000 persons, (mostly people living on charity) took place in May, 1940. Nobody ever heard what became of them.

Jews were forced to do road work, debris clearing, and similar kinds of hard work. Slackers were shot on the spot, especially by an SA gang-leader (Arbeitsfuhrer) with the Christian name Max. He later took over the Jewish firm of Tobiasz, ironmongers, in Sosnowice.

The worst brutes of the Schutzpolizei were Zybis and Miczko, who used to beat up and shoot Jews, and who also employed Jewish informers. The informers blackmailed Jews and then shared the spoils with their police superiors.

Jewish shops and firms were put under the trusteeship of the Volksdeutsche (nationals of Poland, Czechoslovakia, Rumania, who were of German or alleged German origin); most of them came from Upper Silesia. My trustee was a Volksdeutscher from Rumania, with whom I managed to get along quite well. Many of the bigger firms including mine were able to continue their business activities with remarkable success. Officially no Jew was allowed to have more than 1000 marks.

The weekly rations allotted to Jews were very small: about 2 kg bread, and 100 grams of meat which they hardly ever received, some margarine and sugar. People who had not the means to buy extra food from farmers could not exist on these rations.

Work for Jews depended on a permit issued by "Der Sonderbeauftragte fur fremdvolkischen Arbeitseinsatz und Chef der Deutschen SS Polizei in Ost-Oberschlesien," offices in Sosnowice, Rathausstrasse 6. The head of this department was the SS General Schmeldt. The leading officials were SS men Kuczinsky and Nelli, the executive officials were Sturmbannfuhrer Lindner and Scharfuhrer Knoll, both brutes of the worst type. The Jews permitted to work received a blue card when working in a German firm, and a pink one if employed by a Jewish craftsman. For that permit the Jewish employee had to pay 33 percent of his wages or salary, the firm itself an additional 18 to 20 percent of the gross pay, for the privilege of employing the Jew.

With Schmeldt's office the representative body of the Jewish Communities in East Upper Silesia was in constant touch. The Jewish liaison officers were Moses Merin and Usher Kleinberg. To these Jewish Kultusgemeinden belonged Sosnowice, Bendzin, Dombrowa, Strzemeszyce, Olkusz, Zawierczie, Chrzanow, Trzebinia, Wadowice, and some smaller communities. The total figure of Jews living in this district in September, 1939, amounted to at least 100,000 Jews. Through deportations to labor camps in Germany—about 15,000—and deportations to the East with an unknown destination, this figure had decreased by July, 1943, to 30,000.

In the meantime it had leaked out that the deported people had been exterminated in Poland, and everybody tried to save his own life by preparing hiding accommodation. Deep shelters were dug, sometimes with ventilation, the pipes of which were led through trees. Other people tried to buy "Aryan" passports. The majority were very keen on being employed in the official workshops set up by the Jewish Community and working for the German authorities.

Nevertheless, mass deportations took place in summer,

1942, (July or August) when about 6-8,000 were sent to Auschwitz from Bendzin alone. The next mass deportation took place on June 22nd, 1943, followed by the total deportation starting on August 1st, 1943, and lasting for about three days. Only a few Jews were left who managed to hide themselves. Most of them were later discovered and gassed in Auschwitz. On June 22nd my brother Zysman (27 years of age, a bank clerk), his wife Gucia nee Lasker and their 15-month-old daughter were taken to Auschwitz and immediately gassed with the whole group of six to eight thousand.

I was among the transport leaving Bendzin on August 1st. With me were my wife, Halla Lichtenstein, (nee Buchweitz), born 1920, my father-in-law, Pinschas Leib Buchweitz, and his wife, Ita Buchweitz, (nee Schoenberg), aged 51 and 50 years respectively, my brother-in-law, Wolf Buchweitz, a lawyer by profession, aged 30, and a friend, Ella Potock, (nee Niemiez), and another brother-in-law, Moses Buchweitz, aged 28, managing director, and his wife Laura Buchweitz, (nee Lieblich), a teacher of Latin at a high school.

About 3000 people, were loaded into cattle trucks, and arrived after one hour's journey at Auschwitz Camp II. We were dragged out of the trucks and SS men, bellowing, and beating us with clubs and truncheons, drove us to a siding. Here the women were immediately segregated from the men. Parcels had to be thrown on to the ground, and the SS started to select the strong and healthy-looking from the feeble ones. Elderly persons, the feeble-looking ones, and children, were made to jump into 10 or 12 trucks which were waiting. Anyone who would not jump quickly was beaten in the most brutal way, crying children and babies were seized by the SS and their heads bashed against the lorry, or sometimes taken by one foot, like poultry, the head hanging down, and killed by a blow with a club. The sight of these weeping children, with their tear-stained cheeks even more rosy in the summer sun, slaughtered or stunned on the spot, like ducks, broke my heart.

Some parents left their children standing alone, in the hope of saving their own lives, elderly people selected for the trucks tried to get back into the group of the able-bodied, but were brutally dragged out, like my father-in-law, conspicuous by his grey hair.

Beside the trucks, SS men counted the persons loaded on to the vehicles. In a cold, matter-of-fact way they put a stroke in their notebooks for every person flung on the trucks, without noting the names.

The trucks drove off, followed by an ambulance car with the sign of the Red Cross, and returned after a while empty, to be loaded again. Not a single child remained on the assembly square, and of the 3,000 old people of our group, only 450 old were left. On the average, the remainder of each group taken to the camp was 10-15 percent.

We learned later that in the ambulance car there was a case of tins of "CYCLON." These tins were about 15 inches high and about 8 inches in diameter. I had an opportunity of examining such a tin when one day in winter, 1943, rat-killing in some of the huts was carried out. The tins had a yellow label—I forgot the name of the firm, but I know that the stuff was supplied by the I.G.-

Farben concern—with the inscription "For killing vermin, lice, rats, etc." The contents consisted of little blue crystals, which when exposed to the air turned into gas. The prisoners employed in the rat-killing wore gas-masks and opened the tins outside the huts, piercing only a small slit, and then throwing it into the room, which was immediately closed. A poster with a skull warned prisoners against approaching. The effect of the gas was so strong that we block recorders were ordered to stand on guard for 4 hours to warn any prisoner approaching the hut.

The whole group that was brought from Bendzin on the day following my arrival was at once loaded on to the lorries and driven straight to the gas chambers. No selection took place on that day. Many months later I learned the reason for this total extermination of Bendzin Jews. The SS raiding a dug-out in which Jewish members of the underground movement had gone into hiding, threw hand grenades into this strongly defended shelter, whereupon the Jews answered with shots. One or two SS men were supposed to have been killed. For that the chief of Gestapo in Kattowice, Dreier—the other Gestapo official dealing with Jewish affairs was Dr. Mildner—ordered the wholesale extermination of this batch of prisoners.

At first we did not realize where the people on the trucks were driven to. But after we had been marched off—the women separately to the women's camp (FKL-Frauen-Konzentrationslager)—I met in a sort of reception hut a cousin of my wife, who inquired about the fate of my parents-in-law. When he heard of their having been transported on lorries, he said to my brothers-in-law and me: "Now, my boys, you must face the fact that to-day is Jahrzeit (anniversary of death) of your parents. Both are dead, gassed. But keep your chins up and you might come through."

The reception procedure took place in the following order. First, stripping; anyone who tried to keep any of his belongings was warned by the SS that he would be shot. Our hair was then shaved and so were our bodies. As no soap was used and the razors were dirty, in many cases inflammation and skin diseases followed. We were bathed and tattooed on the left forearm, my number was 132564. We were given old, worn-out civilian clothes with a red cross on the back and a red stripe painted on the trouser legs, and on the left side of the chest we had to sew on the Star of David. After the registration of our particulars we were led into the Quarantine Camp, Auschwitz II, Abschnitt A.

Before describing my personal experiences, I should like to give an outline of the Camp of Auschwitz and Birkenau, as the Germans called it, of its administration and of its inmates:

The Camps of Oswiecim, (Auschwitz) and Brze-zinka (Birkenau) and Monowice are actually one large camp, Oswiecim, not more than 1 kilometre from Birkenau, and Monowice about 3 kilometres from Birkenau.

Auschwitz I was the original camp, i.e., Oswiecim proper. There the administrative offices of the camp (the so-called political department, clothing stores, equipment stores), and the camp prison (Bunker) were situated. The prisoners' huts were brick-built; the camp was clean because it served as a kind of show camp.

Auschwitz II, i.e. Birkenau proper, was the death camp. It was divided into a men's and a women's camp. The men's camp was subdivided into

Abschnitt A, Quarantine (16 huts). There the prisoners had a 3-weeks' rest, in order to find out whether they had any infectious diseases, and were then, after examination by SS doctors, detailed for work.

Abschnitt B, the Czech Camp, (32 huts) not meant for Czechs but for Jews from Czechoslovakia, especially from Theresienstadt.

Abschnitt C, Unterkunft, consisting of 32 wooden huts, of which 3 served as store houses. The rest were occupied by prisoners whose identity or nationality I do not know.

Abschnitt D, the so-called "Stammlager" of Auschwitz II, with the main registration and the post office, clothing stores, shoemakers' and tailors' workshops and 32 wooden huts with 12-14,000 prisoners.

Abschnitt E, the gypsy camp. The Germans collected gypsies from all invaded countries, without putting them to work. The little children even received milk and white bread. They were kept there from 1942 till about August 1944, when all of them were gassed.

Abschnitt F, Krankenbau (the Sick Bay), about 32 huts, shunned by everybody because of the constant danger of selection.

Abschnitt G, Neue Sauna, the disinfection and delousing hut for men and women. In the Sauna the closely watched "Filz-Commando" worked, which had to unstitch the civilian garments of the camp inmates and search them for valuables. The same process and the searching of prisoners' luggage took place in huts near the siding where the transports arrived by train. The labour detachment engaged there bore the nickname "Canada-Commando," because people working there were able to wangle provisions and valuables which the deportees had had to give up and were considered wealthy; the SS supervising the "Canada-Commando" enriched themselves by embezzling money, foreign currency, diamonds and provisions taken from the gassed people. Fantastic figures circulated in the camp about the fortunes the SS had made from this kind of business.

Not far from the Sauna, in a little spinney, stood the two horror buildings, each of which contained a gas chamber and six or seven incinerators. Before these two modern death factories had been built, the gassing took place in a little white hut, still standing at the time of my stay in the camp, but no longer used. There were two similar buildings in the women's camp, and three more gas chambers and crematoria which I did not see myself were in some other camps belonging to the Oswiecim establishment.

Prisoners from Auschwitz II used also to work at Harmensee, a big farming estate where especially women were employed in agricultural work.

Auschwitz III, i.e. Monowice, which belonged to the Buna-Werke, controlled by the I.G.-Farben A.G. The building of many factories for the production of synthetic oil and rubber cost thousands of Jewish lives, because of the ill treatment of prisoners engaged in this work at the hands of their guards. The Buna employed subsidiary working detachments in mines and foundries at about 20 places, such as: Guenter-Grube, Fuersten-Grube, Libiaz, Jawoszowice, Jaworzno, Bobrek near Beuthen (German Upper Silesia)—there work was done on behalf of the Siemens-Werke—and Gleiwitz (German Upper Silesia), to which town the detachments were taken by car every morning.

The bulk of the prisoners consisted of Jews, of whom at least three million have passed through the camp. The number of Jews from Germany was very small. I heard that a year before my arrival cars with German Jews from Gleiwitz, Beuthen, Oppeln, Hindenburg and Breslau had been brought to Oswiecim via, Bendzin and Sosnowice where a number of Polish Jews had been added to the transport. Both this group and another one with the remainder of the Silesian Jews, arriving in 1943, were said to have been gassed en masse.

Austrian Jews came from Austrian concentration camps, Jews from the Baltic States, via concentration camp of Stuthoff near Danzig, most of them excellent craftsmen who first did first-class artisans' work and were afterwards gassed. Dutch, Belgian and French Jews joined us, among the latter a strikingly high number of intellectuals, professors, literary men, musicians and officers. A relative of the famous Captain Dreyfus was said to have been among them. Italian, Greek, Czechoslovakian, Hungarian Jews completed the toll, of which, of course, the Polish Jews constituted the majority. Among the Jews from Czechoslovakia I should like to mention especially a transport arriving, if I am not mistaken, in October, 1943, from Theresienstadt, the members of which were not immediately gassed, but put to death after some months rest.

Among the non-Jews there were Poles, Czechoslovakians, Russian civilians, for instance a large batch from Vitebsk, and Russian prisoners of war. The latter had formerly been confined to Stalags, but had been brought to Oswiecim because of their alleged attempts to escape. As soon as Jews among the Russian soldiers were discovered, they were shot at the "black wall," i.e. a wall painted black and splashed with blood. The shooting was mostly done by the SS Oberscharfuehrer Palitsch, commonly known as the best "Genickschuetze" (neck-gunner). At the "black wall" Moses Merin, mentioned earlier, met his end.

In addition, there were German so-called professional criminals and some German political prisoners, Austrians and Yugoslav partisans. From what I heard, I must assume that these partisans had never participated in any kind of guerrilla activities, but were only suspect.

I remember the following names:

Concentration Camp Leader:
Obersturmfuehrer Pollatschek
Sturmbannfuehrer Hess
Sturmbannfuehrer Schwarz
(Rank unknown) Kramer, one of the worst brutes who in spite of his position used to beat up prisoners in the most bestial way and was always foul-mouthed and violent.
Camp Commandants:
Hauptsturmfuehrer Aumeier
Obersturmfuehrer Schwarzhuber

Other ranks:

Hauptscharfuehrer Moll, the murderer of children, one of the vilest murderers, leader of the Camp Gleiwitz in 1944 and 1945 and in charge of Commando Guenter & Fuersten-Grube, about 40 years old, bloated and overfed.

Arbeitsfuehrer Schettel, a beast, about 40 years old, tall and bloated.

Blockfuehrer Scherbinsky, from Lodz, in charge of a detachment at Guenter-Grube, formerly working in the "Political Department" of the camp, always beating up prisoners.

(Rank unknown) Wieczorek, a Volksdeutscher from

Upper Silesia, working in the "Political Department" Auschwitz II.

Oberscharfuehrer Palitsch, the "Genickschuetze."

Dr. Koenig, especially feared because of his ruthlessness in selecting victims.

Dr. Fischer, not as ruthless as all the other doctors; he would listen to the Jewish Dr. Kowacz and spare patients.

Rottenfuehrer Hoffmann, about 30, absolutely ruthless. I head him say: "Now the war has been going on for five years and I cannot understand why the dirty Jews (Dreckjuden) are still alive."

Unterscharfuehrer Frei, Commando-Fuehrer at Guenter-Grube, one of the very few SS men whom I would not consider a sadist. he carried out his orders without inflicting any cruel treatment personally.

From many reports and especially from smuggled letters of my wife, I know that the SS women guards in charge of the women's camp used to kick and whip the women. They were considered at least as vicious as their male counterparts.

I cannot remember having seen SS men with war medals, I don't think any one of them had seen active service.

All of them were, of course, fervent anti-Semites. They

considered everyone opposing Germany and her war as a Jew or at least acting under Jewish influence. Everything English and American, not to speak of Russian Bolshevism, was, according to their abusive talk, Jewish. We noticed that after every address given by Hitler, Ley, Goebbels, etc., the anti-Semitic rage of the SS increased and we were made to feel the consequences. Murder had become a daily routine for them. They would have murdered anybody put into their hands, but for most of them the murdering of Jews seemed to be a special delight. Young guards were drilled to shoot any prisoner overstepping the boundary set for the camp inmates. If they hit they received 14 days' extra leave, and a reward of 30 marks. Sometimes the young guards incited a new prisoner to throw his cap beyond the boundary and then to fetch it, simply in order to shoot him.

The inner administration of the camp was done by prisoners themselves (block seniors, recorders, and "Capos" (gang-leaders). In the women's camp, Slovakian Jewesses assisted the SS women as supervisors. I heard complaints about their treatment of the Jewish women, especially about their embezzling the small food rations due to the prisoners.

EIGHT

A DANCE OF DEATH
AND LIBERATION

Mordecai's story continues:

For three weeks the able-bodied men from my transport, including me, were put into Block 16 belonging to the Quarantine Camp.

We kept the civilian clothes we had received on our arrival, but were left for 6 weeks without any shoes, even wooden ones, which were usually worn by the labour detachments. I became block recorder. Although the stay in the Quarantine was allegedly meant to give newcomers a rest before they were detailed for work, life there was made hell for us. We had to get up at about 4 o'clock and, after roll-call lasting some two to three hours, we got a basin of thin ersatz coffee and at noon 1 litre of a thin soup. Between 4 and 5 p.m. we received 200 grams of bread. That was the whole diet for the day, and everybody suffered after a short while from a starvation psychosis. We were not given any cutlery or plates, but had to eat the soup out of our hands. The day's activities consisted of so-called sports, i.e. drill accompanied by the usual beatings. Besides, we had to do all kinds of road-building work in the precincts of the Quarantine, e.g. levelling. We were chased and beaten up and taught the slogans of the SS:

"You needn't work. You need only say: 'I cannot work,' or 'I don't want to work,' and you'll see what will happen."

"A bullet is too precious for a Jew. To finish off you Jews the electric wire or gas is good enough."
Time and again we heard the saying, "You enter the camp by the gate; you leave it by the chimney."

We saw the daily arrivals, batches of prisoners selected anew, being led to the trucks. We heard the cries of death day and night. We saw women parading naked in front of the SS for selection. At night, we were herded together in rough bunks on which normally 15 people would have had room. But we were at least 30, left without any rugs or blankets, the only protection being our trousers and jackets, which we used as pillows and covers. The whole place was fithy and infested with lice, so that before long many of us had got scabies. People began to envy the dead and many contemplated committing suicide. Some hurled themselves against the electric wire.

After 8 weeks the second selection by an SS doctor and the camp leader took place. Hundreds of prisoners who had become emaciated, in the meanwhile, were chosen for "Sonderbehandlung, SB" special treatment. They were not immediately gassed, but first taken to the so-called "Totenblock" (Death-hut), which did not contain any sanitary convenience. They were not allowed to leave the hut. For three days they received neither food nor drink. During the first two days they remained dressed. On the third day they had to undress and stay completely naked till the afternoon, when they were chased out with clubs and taken to the gas chamber. The whole procedure was deliberately planned in this way to break the victims' last spirit of resistance.

After 6 months' stay in the Quarantine camp I could bear this kind of life no longer, although I had only clerical work to do. But the mental torture, seeing the scenes described all day, and watching the white fumes during the day, and the fiery smoke of the incinerators by night, was too much for me. I applied for transfer to a labor detachment and was detailed to the labor commando Guenter-Grube (Guenthermines), where I first worked as a medical orderly in the HKB—Haeftlings-Krankenbau (prisoners' sick bay) under the supervision of a Jewish doctor from Slovakia, Kovascz.

To apply for admission to this sick bay was very dangerous. Although Dr. Kovascz did everything in his power to help the patients, SS doctors would inspect from time to time, and it was here that most of the victims for SB were selected. When I, in July 1944, had an attack of malaria and my temperature went up to 40.5C (104.9 F), I summoned my last strength to avoid treatment in the sick bay. (I was cured by quinine which, strange as it may seem, I received through the help of an SS man who did not even ask for any payment. He did this favor because he knew me from my service in the clothing stores and had received cigarettes from me. That was the only example of humaneness I ever experienced from the SS)

The prisoners at Guenter-Grube had to do the usual work in the mines. SS guards were only posted at the surface, while in the mines proper, Capos—overseers, themselves prisoners were in command of the gangs. In order to enable the men to do the heavy work, food was much better than in the camp. The prisoners got 2 litres of soup a day, at noon a thick one with peas or potatoes, and the bread ration consisted of 500 grams a day. Twice a week margarine, sausage, cheese or jam, was supplied in addition. Work was continued on Sundays, but in contrast to the camp, every third Sunday was free.

In the summer of 1944, bedsteads, rugs and wood-wool pillows were provided. The SS man Schwarz even suggested that a library might be set up for the use of the prisoners working at Guenter-Grube, and actually some books arrived. But the SS man, Frei kept them for himself.

From the 22nd of February 1944 on I was appointed supervisor in the big clothing store of Guenter-Grube and held this post till October 1944. In this position I had a certain influence, distributing shirts and leather boots and exchanging prisoners' uniforms, and as I kept the store in good order, the "Prominencia," i.e. the old prisoners in superior jobs, and even the SS respected the work done by me. I was able to communicate with my wife in the women's camp.

Prisoners working in labor detachments, in which they came into contact with civilians outside the camps, brought me news, especially the B.B.C. news or at least the reports of the German High Command. They brought, through the good offices of civilians, cigarettes, spirits and food into the camp. A lively trade went on all the time, in spite of the severest penalties. Some prisoners, especially those in the so-called "Filz-Commando" who had to search the civilian clothes taken from the inmates for valuables, were in possession of money, even of dollars, and diamonds. There was also barter trading in provisions, e.g. a tin of sardines for a good shirt, etc. Anyone who did not participate in the wangling to procure some additional food would not have been able to survive. I was particularly anxious to supply my wife with food and medical requirements; she urgently needed injections when typhus broke out in the women's camp and I was able to procure them for her.

In the camp slang this clandestine trade, by which the SS too made huge sums of money, was called "Organisieren"—organizing. When a new camp senior, a Bavarian prisoner named Ludwig, a politician who had spent 11 years in several concentration camps, took over the post of the camp senior, he forbade any kind of "organizing." I was transferred to a labor gang and started leading a group whose job it was to push heavy iron trucks. I held this post till we were evacuated. This was just sham work, because we had to push the trucks to a site where factories were to be built. Actually, building was impossible owing to the frost, and although no work was done by the bricklayers, we had to start at 6:30 in the morning and finish pushing the trucks at half past four.

We were not allowed to warm ourselves at a fire. Anyone who did so was beaten up and punished by extra drill after the evening roll-call. This kind of sham occupation was only done in order to keep us on the run.

In November, 1943, about 1500 non-Jewish prisoners from the German concentration camps Gross-Rosen and Flossenburg arrived in Auschwitz, all of them Russians or Poles, completely emaciated and resembling living skeletons. First we heard that they were to have a rest in the Quarantine camp, but towards the evening the SS ordered the hut seniors to "finish them off." As non-Jews were hardly ever gassed, this order meant that the hut seniors had to use whatever means were at their disposal to murder these poor wretches. They were taken to Huts 3 and 11, and some of the worst brutes among the hut seniors gave them, still clothed, a cold shower in the bathhouse. Then they threw most of them who were too weak to walk outside the hut and left them in a heap to their fate. In the morning about 400-500 were dead, frozen to death. I and some other block recorders tried to save as many as possible by smuggling them into the huts where we gave them food. Even so, many of them died from exhaustion.

On a Sunday in January, 1944, we saw cars loaded with naked woman, whom we had heard screaming since 5 o'clock in the morning, prepared for the trip to the gas chamber. It was during roll-call at 10 o'clock a.m. when we, standing to attention in our groups, saw the cars move off. One of the naked girls jumped from a car, clutched the boot of an SS man and cried: "Let me live, I am so young!" The SS man pulled his boot free and smashed her skull by violently trampling on it. We in our files were not allowed to move a muscle, but I noticed that the Russian prisoners-of-war clenched their fists in despair and rage. The dead body was flung on to the truck, and the SS man put a stroke in his notebook.

On another Sunday in that same month, Hauptsturm-fuehrer Schwarzhuber, two SS doctors and two SS men, ordered us to parade, and the numbers of 6-7,000 people were put down for special treatment (SB). This time even healthy-looking men were among the victims, and I too came in for consideration. Schwarzhuber looked at me and, by a lucky chance which I cannot explain, waved me aside. Afterwards one of the doctors came into one of the huts in which the selected people had been placed without shoes, standing on a concrete floor. With the utmost cynicism, but with assumed solicitude, he warned the men against the cold and ordered them to put on their shoes at once and to shut the doors so that they might not catch a chill. He knew, of course, well enough that these selected prisoners were condemned to die in three days' time.

While scenes of this kind were going on day and night, the camp administration insisted on theatre and concert arrangements by the prisoners. Jewish actors from Vilna and Vienna had to give performances, even operettas, and the SS were among the audience. The working parties were led to their assigned places of work while a prisoners' band was playing at the gate, and when they returned to the camp the band again played gay music. Nearly every night any labor detachment would bring with it 40-50 dead people, worked to death or beaten to death. The gangs had to carry back their dead, because the number of the returning prisoners had to correspond to the number that had left the camp in the morning. Alive or dead, the number had to agree.

Starving camp mates had to stand to attention, looking at the smoke of the crematoria, but the band went on playing and we had to sing the jolly camp songs, "Lore, Lore," "The Swiss Maiden" and "Westerwald," as the spirit of the prisoners had to be kept up, in the words of the SS cynics.

In January 1944 a famous Jewish actor from Vilna, whose name I forget, was among the selected. He implored the SS man Kurpanik to spare him, pointed to his physical strength and to his usefulness for hard work. "You know, I am an artist and you have appreciated my art." Kurpanik listened, not without sympathy, but declared himself unable to do anything, as the actor's number had been put down for SB Finally, the actor begged him to do him a last favor and shoot him down. Kurpanik asked him to run, which the actor did, whereupon the SS man fired some shots after him without, however, hitting him. The actor turned, tore his jacket open and shouted "Shoot now!" This bullet reached its goal.

One night in June 1944 we were ordered out for a special roll call, and four Jews, my brother-in-law Moses Buchweitz among them, were taken by car to the "Political Department." It leaked out that they were being tried by the SS for an alleged attempt to escape. For six weeks we lived in an atmosphere of frightful suspense. At the end of July or in early August some carpenters and I had to build a gallows for five persons. The next morning the names of Jidel Pottock, Heniek Ehrenfried, Moses Buchweitz and that of a fourth man whose name I cannot remember were called. They heard their death-sentences pronounced in Polish and German and were asked to state whether they had understood the sentence. When they answered in the affirmative in a low voice they were made to repeat, shouting, "Jawohl" and hanged.

The actual killing in the gas chambers took place in the following way. In front of the chambers, people had to alight from the lorries, or were simply tipped out by means of a winch. Sometimes they were given a towel and a piece of soap, driven into the chambers and beaten if resisting, supposedly to take a bath and be deloused. Then the doors were shut and screwed down.

By an electrical process the air was pumped out. An SS man opened a trap-door near the roof, about 40 centimeters square, and threw one or several tins of CYCLON into the gas chamber. If a sufficient quantity of the substance was used, asphyxiation was complete in about 3 to 5 minutes. Otherwise the killing was said to have lasted 25 to 30 minutes. The Jewish electricians working in the crematoria told me that the SS had several times not used a sufficient amount of gas and that the "Sonder-Commando" people, Jews, employed in removing the victims had found the corpses clutched fast together in the final agony of suffocation.

The "Sonder-Commando" had great difficulty in separating the bodies. Through a peephole covered by thick glass SS doctors watched the gassing and then ordered the automatic ventilation of the chambers. Now the "Sonder-Commando," about 200 men, pulled the corpses out of the place. The hair of the victims was then shorn, their gold and metal teeth broken out of their mouths. On little carts the corpses were taken to the crematoria, where they were burned by an electrical current of 6,000 volts. Most of the people were sent to this death completely naked, but if the incoming transports were too big and the SS wanted to hurry things up, they were killed in their clothes. The "Sonder-Commando" had to undress them afterwards.

For gassed people no death certificate was issued, but those inmates who died in the sick bay, or were shot, had their certificate drawn up. As the cause of death, various reasons were given, such as pneumonia, heart trouble, or "shot while trying to escape." I need not stress that all of these doctor's certificates were false.

Of scientific experiments on prisoners, I know only that young Jews, men and women, were forcibly sterilized. When they returned to our huts pale and bewildered they told us about their sad experience.

On the 18th of January, 1945, at 10 p.m. our detachment at the Guenter-Grube, about 560 men, had to assemble for roll-call and were given marching orders. At first we thought that now our turn had come and that we were to be gassed. So I told an SS man, Franek by name, a Croat, that I would not submit to being gassed, but rather would prefer a bullet. I urged him to tell me the truth and he finally told me that we were not to be gassed, but to be transported westwards. From all the other work detachments similar batches of prisoners were marched off.

Awaiting liberation.

Dachau, probably the most horrifyingly obscene of all the concentration camps. It is estimated over a quarter of a million bodies were burned in its furnaces. When the Allied soldiers liberated those still alive they found thousands of bodies piled high waiting to be cremated. Prisoners in various states of disbelief welcomed the Americans even as they seized their former SS jailers and killed and tossed their bodies in the ditches to lay beside their executed comrades.

At Belsen concentration camp women were forced to strip the bodies of the executed before they were cremated.

...Over 60,000 prisoners suffered and died from typhus, dysentery and typhoid.

...German women guards were as unremitting in their brutality as their male counterparts

At the Guenter-Grube, however, about 20 sick prisoners who were not able to walk were left behind. They, together with 160 fellow-prisoners, were packed into the Fuerstengrube sick bay and the whole hut was burnt down.

Many of the party were too weak to stand the strain of this march all through the night and the following day, which led us through Tichy, Mikolow to Mocry. Anyone who broke down on the road was shot on the spot. We passed hundreds of bodies lying by the roadside. Some of the fellows were only wounded and implored us to take them with us. But we could not do that. I dragged my brother Jakob, who had come to Oswiecim in September 1943, on my arm. Although I have seen death a thousand times and have become somewhat callous, I must say that the sight of the poor fellows lying in the bloodstained snow, desperately begging for pity and help, is the most horrible impression which haunts my mind.

Some of us were made to draw big sledges, normally drawn by horses, on which the SS took their kit and equipment with them.

I arrived in Gleiwitz (German Upper Silesia) on Saturday, January 20th at 4 a.m. For nearly two days we had not had any food and hardly any water. We were taken to the camp Gleiwitz 1 where we were to spend the night.

Some of my comrades discovered potatoes and on an improvised brick stove they started cooking them. The SS shot some bullets into the party, but we were much too hungry to discontinue eating. At 10 a.m., we were marched off, but had to return to the camp because of an English or American air-raid. During the day and the night we had to stand in the camp without being given any food or drink.

On Sunday at 10 a.m. we were again marched off to the station, and everyone not able to walk was ordered to report for transport by ambulances. We did not believe that ambulances had been provided for us, but to our great surprise ambulance cars were waiting in one of the main roads of Gleiwitz. That was done deliberately, because the SS wanted to stage a show for the people of Gleiwitz who were just returning from church and were to see how humanely prisoners were treated. But on the station, we, the able-bodied, were driven with truncheons into open coal wagons, about 200-250 men being herded in one wagon. Many fell down, unconscious, from hunger and exhaustion. In my wagon we had three or four dead. Some hundreds of sick ones who had made the journey to the station in the ambulance cars, were shot near Gleiwitz.

The transport, about 4000 men, left Gleiwitz at night, but stopped after the train had travelled about 15 kilometres. At Regisfeld the train remained the whole night at the station. We asked the engine drivers where we could find some water. Anyone who tried to quench his thirst was shot at, but, fortunately, not everyone was hit.

On Monday, the 22nd, at 2 p.m., we started marching along a country road leading through deep forests in the direction of Laband.

Every few yards we saw dead comrades lying by the

roadside, all of them shot. I was convinced that we were not to survive this nightmare march. Suddenly the SS opened fire. I darted into the forest, dropping to the ground to take cover. At least 2000 were shot and killed.

After the firing had ceased and I was about to rise I saw an SS man in front of me aiming his gun and saying, "You swine, you wanted to escape." I denied it, and told him that I was one of the sledge party and had to take cover. The SS man was satisfied and left me and 10 other Jews under the guard of an elderly sentry, who did not belong to the SS. He must have been a member of the Wehrmacht, but I could not make out his uniform.

Between the main batch of the prisoners and our sledge party there was a gap which I tried to extend 'til we could not see the marchers any longer. A young Jew who could not stand the strain of hauling the heavy sledge any longer suddenly tore open his jacket and begged the guard to shoot him. I shouted at him not to be a fool and give up just at the last moment, but he explained that he was suffering from tuberculosis and would not survive this march. The guard did not shoot him and the boy had to go on marching.

From a conversation between our guard and a German policeman on a motor-bike, I gathered that we were near Sumina and Zupowice and that we were to be taken to Ratibor. The policeman, inquiring whether there were a great number of corpses by the roadside, recommended a shorter route to Ratibor through the woods. I had made up my mind to take the first opportunity of escaping and hiding till the Russians should approach. I explained to our guard that we had not had any food or drink for some days and persuaded him to allow us to ask a farm woman we saw for some water. The woman gave us buckets of water and bread while the farmer offered some buttered bread to the guard. He did not, however, accept it, so I took it and distributed it among my comrades.

I noticed that the farm people spoke Polish, although the Upper Silesian population talks both German and Polish. From that I inferred that they too were expecting the Russians. Near Rauden we again passed some farm houses where the women were waiting with filled buckets. Our guard forbade us to drink, whereupon about 20 women hurled themselves at him and heaped abuse on him: "Have you never heard of a "Tierschutzverein" (Association for the Protection of Animals)? No decent man would refuse water to an animal, and you...." We nevertheless were not permitted to drink, because as the guard, somewhat ashamed, explained afterwards, we had to hurry to Ratibor.

In the Rauden forest I noticed a slope where we had to stop because the guard wanted to relieve himself. He hung his rifle on a tree and retired. I used this moment to seize the rifle which I threw down the slope, and then flung myself down it too. I called to my comrades in Yiddish: "After me, but everyone on his own responsibility." Only one French Jew followed me. I saw the guard march the others off.

We stayed in the forest for a long time and then approached a farmhouse, where I talked to an old farmer in Polish. His daughter gave us coffee with sugar, the first coffee I had had for years, and then sent us to the barn of another farmer where we spent the night. In the morning, women entered the barn chattering, so that they did not notice the French Jew's snoring.

After a while a soldier in a green uniform with a rifle came into the barn, heard the snoring man, aimed his gun at the spot where we were lying under the straw, and ordered us to come out. He took us to the road where long columns of the German army were resting. He reported our case to his officer, and asked for orders as to what to do with these two escaped prisoners. The officer's answer was very short: "Well, let them go." We ran away and after the columns had disappeared, we went back to the farmhouse. The farmer's daughter gave me a razor and at my request some good socks. When asked from whom she had this men's outfit she told me that there were English prisoners-of-war nearby.

I went straight to the little camp where 22 English, Australian and New Zealand prisoners were doing forestry work. The chaps, to whom I spoke in German, gave me a tremendous welcome. I suggested becoming their interpreter in case the Russians should approach, an event which we might occur at any hour. From that day on I had the time of my life, although the Germans were still about.

On the 26th of January, at 7 a.m., we heard machine-gun fire in the woods and then I saw the scene which I had envisaged a hundred times in all those years of suspense: Russian tanks breaking through, firing all the time. I led the party of 22 British prisoners 'til we met a Russian major, who aimed his gun at us. I explained that we were not Germans, as he supposed, but all British. The British chaps had meanwhile given us cardigans and decent trousers, so that the two of us no longer looked like prisoners from the concentration camp. The major sent us back behind the front, and after some wandering, always being challenged by Russian patrols, we reached Gross-Strehlitz. The slogan, "We are British, Churchill, Roosevelt and Stalin are allies, comrades-in-arms," made the Russians very friendly. They gave us wine, vodka, and once even a whole pig. We were sent back to Czenstochova, an assembly point for Allied prisoners-of-war.

In Czenstochova I acted as interpreter for about 250 British prisoners-of-war who were to be sent home by the Russian authorities. As the British and I had become great friends, they suggested that I might go with them to this country though I would have had an opportunity of being sent to Palestine. With the British I was evacuated to this country via Cracow, Odessa, Port Said and Gilbraltar.

Before I left Poland I wanted to see Bendzin for a last time. I wish I had not returned to ths once flourishing Jewish town which has now become a ghost town. Of 30,000 Jews living there five and a half years ago, only 160 were registered on February 15th, 1945 and I assume that even these figures are too high. For beggars might have gone from one place to another and registered at each of them.

Now I am here, I live [in 1945] in the elegant flat of a friend from Bendzin, I am free, but I cannot feel happy. My parents-in-law were gassed, my younger brother, his wife and their little daughter gassed, my brother-in-law

Moses hanged, and his wife and her friend died from typhus in the women's camp. I lost sight of my second brother and my brother-in-law, Wolf, during the shooting near Laband, and I do not know whether they have survived that assault. Worst of all, however, I do not know anything about my wife's fate. I only know that the women were evacuated from Auschwitz like ourselves and taken across the Oder.

I am very grateful for the hospitality Britain has offered me, but whether a man of my experience will ever be able to enjoy life again, that remains to be seen. At the moment I cannot believe it.

NINE

RESISTANCE, REVOLT AND MASSACRE

L ate in May 1942, Reinhard Heydrich, deputy chief of the Gestapo and Hitler's chief enforcer of the *Final Solution,* was assassinated by two Czechoslovak rebels while driving in his Mercedes sports car. After hurling a British-made bomb into the car of "the Hangman" (as Heydrich had come to be known), they made their way to a church where they sought refuge. Several days after Heydrich died of his wounds, the SS found the church and killed the two assassins along with 120 members of the Czech resistance.

Although Heydrich's slayers were not Jewish, it was the Jews who suffered most because of his death. Nearly three thousand Jews were removed from the so-called "elite" ghetto of Theresienstadt and sent to extermination camps. In the small village of Lidice, not far from Prague, hundreds of German security police, under the command of Captain Max Rostock (who was eventually hanged in Prague in 1951), surrounded the community without warning. Within twenty-four hours the entire male population (nearly 200) was executed. The women, including children, were sent to a concentration camp where they were gassed. Lidice was no more!

On October 28, 1941, twenty-six thousand Jews of the Kovno ghetto in Lithuania marched before the SS. After weeks of terror, indiscriminate shootings, forced labor which usually resulted in death, rape and murder of the town's women, and torture, the Germans told the Jewish community that they would be divided into those who could do heavy labor for the Reich and those who, unable to work, would be sent to another "settlement." Although the majority of the population knew what this order really meant, few wanted to believe its consequences. Still, it was decided by the Jews that if they didn't comply with the German order to assemble, they would *all* be killed. Therefore, to save a few, community elders decided to obey German orders.

Jewish families were separated. The very young and elderly were directed in one direction, the rest formed another line. The next day some ten thousand Jews, unfit for work, were marched outside the city limits and shot.

The question is still asked: why did the Jews not resist the Germans, especially in the face of certain death? The fact is there was organized Jewish resistance. But what is even more remarkable is the fact that the Jews were able t organize *any* resistance at all.

As the Germans marched through eastern Europe, whole armies of well-trained soldiers were crushed and annihilated by the Nazi war machine. How then were civilians, poorly armed and untrained, supposed to counter the Gestapo and SS? There was no such thing as civil disobedience against the Germans, for civil disobedience requires a "moral" government which will accept protest without inflicting death on innocent and accused alike. Further, the Germans played on the anti-Semitic nature of much of the eastern European non-Jewish population, who, in order to save themselves, were all too eager to help the Germans rid their communities of the *Judenrat.*

Unlike the rest of the civilian population, Jews were faced with the problem of *total* extermination by the Nazis. The dual aim of those Jews who were able to resist the Germans was not only to disrupt the German war effort, but to save as many Jews from extermination as possible.

Jewish resistance began in the large ghettos which were sealed off by the Germans, particularly Warsaw, Vilna, and Bialystok. It also existed in all other occupied German territory, from France to Russia. Jews joined the partisan struggle along with other underground brigades, some of which were supported by their government-in-exile. At the war's conclusion no one knows how many thousands of Jewish partisans had fought the Germans. But it was only a fraction of those who *wished* to do so.

From the moment each ghetto was formed, Jews faced great obstacles in terms of organized resistance. First, the occupying Germans were constantly on the lookout for Jewish political leaders. They were taken away at once when located. There was always the threat of mass murder should ghetto residents openly resist. As long as the Germans gave hope to the Jewish citizens, which they often did, few wanted to actively resist. In the Lodz ghetto, for example, where thousands of Jews worked for German industry, there was no armed resistance, despite the deportation of children, the old and sick to extermination camps.

Ghetto Jews faced another obstacle. In order for any resistance group to be effective, its efforts needed Allied coordination. At the beginning of the war Great Britain was the only nation partisans could rely on. Sealed off in the ghetto, the Jews were unable to receive any outside instruction, or financial and military aid.

In the ghetto, two views regarding resistance emerged. The first held that Jews should remain in the ghetto and fight the Germans, even though their efforts would be more symbolic than meaningful in terms of halting the extermination process. The second notion was to abandon the ghetto for the forest where they might join the Russian-supported resistance fighters.

In Vilna, where the first major Jewish resistance was organized in January of 1942, the *United Partisans Organization* (UPO) was founded by some 150 young Zionists. It was decided first that, after destroying ghetto buildings and blowing up German ammunition depots, they would retreat to the woods. However, unable to fulfill their original goals, they moved to the forest where they joined with Soviet partisans.

Shortly after their formation, the UPO issued its first underground official proclamation. It read in part, "Let us not go like sheep to the slaughter....Of eighty thousand Jews in the 'Jerusalem of Lithuania' only twenty thousand survive.

"—Where are the hundreds of Jews who were taken away for work by the Lithuanian kidnappers?

"—Where are the naked women and the children who

were taken from us during the awful night of the provocation?

"...Hitler aims to destroy *all* the Jews of Europe.

"...Brothers! Better to fall as free fighters than to live at the mercy of the murderers.

"Let us revolt! We shall fight until our last breath."

Despite the truth of their warning, the Vilna partisans had a difficult time convincing a large portion of the population that they should rise up against the Germans. They were able, however, to arouse the spirit of enough young Jews to become an effective guerrilla force.

In June of 1942, the Vilna partisans carried out the first of many important diversionary actions against the Germans. After securing a powerful explosive device, several patisians waited near a crossing for a German transport train. As the train passed over the device, the partisans set it off, causing a tremendous explosion and derailing dozens of cars. Continuous bursts of fire racked the remaining cars. Partisan scouts confirmed that at least two hundred German soldiers were killed, with many more wounded. This was the UPO's first sabotage action of the war. At the time, these Jews were still mainly confined to the ghetto, which made their action even more remarkable.

As the UPO continued to grow in strength, it began to receive outside help. In August of 1942, along with other partisan units, the UPO was taken in under the umbrella of Soviet organization which headed the Central Staff of the Partisan Movement. Their specific job was to harass the rear flank of the German army.

In September of 1943 groups of UPO fighters formed the Jewish Brigade which was made up of four battalions under the command of Abba Kovner. Members of the

Kovno underground helped make up the Lithuanian Brigade, which was nearly all Jewish.

By the end of 1943 the forests surrounding the large eastern European ghettos were filled with numerous partisan organizations. Their main objectives were to destroy German transport trains before they could reach the front as well as offer resistance against German troops whenever possible.

By mid-1943 the German High Command was quite concerned over partisan activity along the Eastern front. Goebbels, in his diary of the war years 1942-43, makes note of the partisan threat. "An SD report informed me about the situation in occupied Russia...The Partisan danger is increasing week by week. The Partisans are in command of large areas in occupied Russia and are conducting a regime of terror there. The national movements, too, have become more insolent that (sic) was first imagined...Everywhere the Jews are busy inciting and stirring trouble."

Jewish partisans from Vilna were not the only heroic freedom fighters among the Jewish population. The story of the Warsaw ghetto uprising is also one of valiant Jewish effort against insurmountable odds.

By the spring of 1943 all that was left of the 400,000 Jews herded by the Nazis into the Warsaw ghetto was 60,000. The rest of the population had been exterminated by the Germans.

Since the Germans sealed off the ghetto in 1940, those Jews that remained fought a daily battle against starvation (most were able to eat no more than a watery bowl of soup, often boiled with straw), disease and deportation to the concentration camps. Apparently the Germans felt the ghetto would liquidate itself through attrition. It did not. The Warsaw Jewish underground (Left Labor Zionist Jews), a political party which undertook to oversee underground military activities and called its organization *Zydowska Organizacja Bojowa* (ZOB: Jewish Combat Organization), was more effective in maintaining order, hope and resistance than the Germans suspected. Hundreds of Jewish partisans lived in underground hideouts, some of which actually had running water, or access to deep wells, relatively large food stocks, electricity and even homemade radios, which were used to monitor Allied activity.

By 1943 long networks of underground passageways ran from one building to another. The Germans, who eventually came to realize they were being eluded by hundreds of Jews, publicly offered food and other inducements to pull the Jews from their hideouts. The ZOB was quick to counter the German offers with stern reminders that the penalty for coming forward would be the informer's own death.

Among other problems, the Jewish underground constantly faced the problem of Gestapo informers within their ranks. However, with the increasing efficiency of their organization German spies, when discovered, were swiftly liquidated by the ZOB.

The first major military test for the ZOB came in January of 1943. Himmler paid a surprise visit to the ghetto that month and, to his dismay, found that too many Jews were left in the ghetto. He ordered the SS officer in charge, Major General of the Police Juergen Stroop, to complete "resettlement" by February of that year.

On January 18th German troops surrounded the ghetto in an attempt to begin final clearing action.

Unable to communicate among themselves and taken completely by surprise, five separate ZOB fighting units, armed with rifles, a few grenades and several machine guns responded to the German threat by killing and wounding at least 50 Germans, plus recovering some of their weapons. Despite their own heavy losses, the ZOB managed to halt the German deportation effort.

With morale high, the ZOB reorganized itself with the help of the ZKK (*Zydowski Komitet Koordynacyjny:* Jewish Coordinating Committee), a separate but allied underground political group. Preparing for the inevitable, the ZOB organized itself in fighting units of ten, each unit consisting of at least two women. The total by March of 1943 was twenty-two units. In that same month the ZOB rooted out virtually every Gestapo agent within their ranks. After killing five, they passed out leaflets warning other German agents that they had their names and would deal with them in similar fashion.

Three days after their successful actions against the Germans, the ZOB sent a radio message to the Polish government-in-exile in London. In part the message read;

"We notify you of the greatest crime of all times, about the murder of millions of Jews in Poland...We ask you:

"Revenge against the Germans...Fight for our lives and our honor.

"Brothers—the remaining Jews in Poland live with the awareness that in the most terrible days of our history you did not come to our aid. Respond, at least in the last days of our life."

Desperate to liquidate the Warsaw ghetto without threat to their own soldiers, the Germans placed a Polish owner of a factory which employed 8,000 ghetto Jews in charge of inducing them to come forward placidly for resettlement. The Jews were told they would be sent to a camp with ideal living conditions.

Shortly after the announcement was made, the ZOB blew up the factory. Of the 8,000 employees, only twenty-five showed up to accept the German offer.

By April of 1943 the Germans began running out of patience. On the 19th of that month, they sent nearly 2,000 heavily armed SS troops into Warsaw to clear out the ghetto. Again, they were surprised by heavy resistance. Using Molotov cocktails, rifles and automatic weapons, the ZOB managed to stop several German tanks and kill or wound upwards of 200 German troops. Stunned by the heavy resistance, the Germans withdrew their attack.

In his diary of the events which led to Jewish resistance in the Warsaw ghetto, General Stroop reported his amazement at their strong resistance. "Whereas it had been possible during the first days to catch considerable number of Jews, who are cowards by nature, it became more and more difficult...to capture the bandits and Jews. Over and over again new battle groups consisting of 20 to 30 Jewish men, accompanied by a corresponding number of women, kindled new resistance."

By April 24th, the fifth day of a battle (which Himmler had ordered ended within three days), Stroop reported the capture of some 27,000 Jews. This was accomplished mostly by the use of massive fires set by the Germans throughout the ghetto. Entire blocks were reduced to ashes, as fleeing Jewish resistance fighters were captured or killed by the Germans.

By the end of the first week in May the Germans located the ZOB command center. Instead of forcefully rooting them out the Germans blocked up the entrance after sending poisonous gas inside. Many of the fighters committed suicide. Some, however, managed to make their way through the underground Warsaw sewers to safety.

By the 16th of May the fighting came to an end. The Jewish ghetto in Warsaw had been virtually liquidated. Hardly a building remained intact. The resistance action led to an inferno which resulted in the death of some 56,000 remaining Jews. Those who were not killed escaped to the forest or managed to live in occupied communities under assumed Aryan identities.

For all practical purposes, Jewish life and tradition had been wiped out in Poland. Those who remained, constantly chased, harassed and in perpetual fear of discovery by the Gestapo, nevertheless remained alive to bear witness to the Holocaust.

The Warsaw resisters not killed by the Germans were ent to Treblinka where they would be gassed along with other inmates. However, once resistance fighters, their spirit lingered, even in this, one of the most notorious of all concentration camps. In August of 1943, along with other inamates, the ghetto freedom fighters staged a brief revolt inside Treblinka. Some still had revolvers and hand grenades and, on a given signal, after their arrival, they opened fire on the guards and set the camp on fire. After murdering the guards, they raided the German arsenal, stole more weapons and ocntinued to slaughter the German troops stationed there. Having caused total havoc, they escaped into the surrounding forest.

Unfortuntely the Germans were ble to root out most of the Jews and execute them. Of the 700 inmates involved in the uprising, only a dozen or so managed to elude the

Germans.

Treblinka was not the only camp to suffer insurrection. At Auschwitz a small revolt broke out among the prisoners and, before it was squelched, they managed to destroy three crematoria. This revolt, too, was ultimately unsuccessful, as the Jews involved in the uprising were put to death.

In 1939 it was estimated that nearly ten million Jews lived in territories eventually occupied by the Reich. Hitler carried out the *Final Solution* almost until the very end of the war.

TEN

NOTES FROM UNDERGROUND
AND LIBERATION

What follows are accounts of what it was like under Nazi oppression. How easily words are used. How incomplete they are, how inadequate words are, as Shelley observed, but the only tools we have. There has been an attempt to integrate the history of those times, the facts as reported and annotated with the accounts of some of the survivors. What one has as a result is the perception of truth of those who lived through the years of the *Final Solution* and the perception of truth of those who record the acts. In some instances they mesh; in others they may differ. But it is the perception which is true. And although there may be variances, there is a greater truth to all of the accounts.

How simple is the truth of one man who tells of the events after the fall of 1938, when all the male members of his community were ordered by the Gestpo to appear at the local police station. How unemotional are the words now: "After I had left my residence the SS and the SA came and broke up everything I had, turned over the cupboards, slit open the beds and sprinkled acid on the carpets."

And then there is the simple phrase that, before leaving "they hurt my wife."

What does that phrase imply—to the writer, to the reader? The soldiers looted the stores, burned the synagogue and the holy artifacts.

The Jews who were arrested were sent to Buchenwald by "Special Transport." Barracks which were designed to hold 20,000, in less than a week contained in excess of 60,000 prisoners. "We had to stay out in the cold and rain for hours without food and drink and no one was allowed to fall out."

Later food and drinking water were at a premium with much less than was necessary for bare survival. Epidemics broke out, killing those the Germans did not. An electrified fence surrounded the camp and many of the inmates went to their death on that fence "out of desperation."

Prisoners slept six or eight to a bunk. They had insufficient clothing against the cold. There was no hospital. "The sick prisoners were placed in a former laundry and left there to perish." After signing an agreement to sell all of his property the writer of these notes was discharged. The letter and the sale were fakes. He received no money, of course. "I also was told that if I ever spoke to anyone about my experience at Buchenwald I would be arrested again."

Then, in a turn of events which has been consistent by its irrationality, the prisoner was released and told to report at Gestapo headquarters. His property was taken away. He received his Jewish identity card. The time was early winter of 1939. The Holocaust was born and quickly approaching maturity.

"Jew" on one's ration card meant not being sold

merchandise. Hours of shopping were limited. "Once every month the Gestapo made a search of all Jewish residences and took away anything they liked."

In 1942 began the "East transports, to Auschwitz, Lublin."

The writer and his wife were sent to Theresienstadt—a ghetto state. Here mostly old and sick Jews "governed" themselves. "The young and healthy were sent to work and perish in Polish death chambers." But he and his wife were eventually liberated by the Russians. He had been sent to the ghetto with fifty others. He was the only one to come out of the Holocaust alive.

No killings remembered in writing here, no slaughter of the innocents graphically described. There are no written recollections of bodies dumped in ditches, of naked bodies waiting to be exterminated, of screams and shouts. It is a rather stilted account of six years of skirting death, of existing, of wondering, of seeing the unspeakable and the unrepeatable. And in that last may be an answer—that the horrors, for some, simply cannot be articulated.

Or this writer, who can articulate and does remember. It was during the Nazi occupation of Lwow when the Ukrainian militia was given permission to round up all the Jewish intellectuals, to have them murdered. Years later this man would reject the offer of friendship of a former Ukrainian friend who had joined the Ukrainian Nazi group. "Those are tragic dilemmas," he wrote, "you face in tragic times. Human beings are mixtures of good and evil and you don't know whom or when to reject. We faced the same situation later when Polish friends had saved our lives. Yet the majority of Poles tolerated or enjoyed the extermination of Polish Jewry by the Nazis."

And the now-familiar story repeats itself, as the Jews were forced into a ghetto. "Any unauthorized Jewish presence outside the ghetto was punishable by death. Terror reigned in the streets of the ghetto. Jewish life had become a cheap commodity...Three possibilities wee left to Jews in those macabre days of the catastrophe: 1) to hope against hope for some miraculous salvation and face death in one way or another, sooner or later; 2) to escape by committing suicide, and many chose that role; 3) to risk or save your life by hiding or assuming a Polish name and playing the role of the gentile 'Aryan.' "

The writer tried to work in the ghetto, but work meant cooperating and "final death in any case." The decision was made to hide, to leave one's family. "However I could no longer take life in the ghetto and anything, including a faster death, appeared to me preferable."

This, taken from an unpublished letter, is a story of forged birth certificates, faked marriage licenses, friends who recognized them but made no outcry of identification. It is a tale of contact with an underground organization that arranged employment, living accomodations, of avoiding Gestapo searches.

These were Jews who monitored allied broadcasts, who lived "good Christian lives." They worked in the underground even as the Jews were being exterminated in Treblinka, as the Warsaw Ghetto was destroyed. They could see the emaciated faces and bodies of children. Gradually hearing news of the liquidation of the members of one's family—and the underground work went on. And liberation! Liberation from what, to be a nonperson for over two years, in displaced persons camps. And trying to get to Palestine or a visa for the U.S. and coming up against a system of quotas that defied reason. But up to the time of liberation Jews had been fighting back—had come up from underground.

As the Russian army had closed in on the Nazi-occupied city of Vilna in the summer of 1944, the Germans remained to stage a stubborn defense of that area. Along with other resisters, Jewish partisans were assigned to Soviet army units to help flush out German troops within the city limits. Acting as guides, they led the Russians inside the city, an act of great service to the Russian soldiers.

After several days of heavy fighting, with terrible losses on both sides, the Russian army, with the help of Jewish partisans, prevailed. Returning to civilian life, many of the partisans attempted o rebuild what they had lost.

In a note of official recognition, the Soviet Lithuanian President, Yustas I. Paleckis, said in July of 1945;

"The Jews of Vilna wrote a heroic chapter in the history of Judaica of Vilna with the story of the struggle of the Vilna Jews against the German occupation forces. Jews did not go to their death passively; they fought bravely against the German aggressor."

By war's end Lublin, Poland became a city Jews would always remember. Piror to German occupation it had been a mecca for Jewish learning. After Germany's invasion of Poland, they turned this city into the center of some 50 concentration camps which surrounded it, among them, Treblinka, Sobibor, and Maidenek. Maidenek had the horrific distinction of gassing more Jews in one day than any other camp: 17,000 in one twenty-four hour period, on November 3, 1943.

As the Allies liberated concentration camps which surrounded Lublin, as well as other parts of eastern Europe, victims of the Holocaust neither jumped for joy nor embraced their liberators. For the most part, they were too weak, too sick, too mentally anguished to respond at all.

In April of 1945 as the Allies approached Buchenwald, for example, the SS attempted to erase all evidence of the camp's horror. Camp inmates were told to supply 3,000 people immediately for transport. To disobey the order would have meant instant annihilation of the entire camp. In order to prevent premature liquidation, camp elders selected 3,000 of their own to meet death in order that the rest might live a little longer.

Actions such as these placed a terrible strain on the survivors. Many felt guilty because they, unlike their friends and families, actually lived through the Holocaust. For the most part, their survival was due not to great cunning, but the will to survive and extreme good fortune: in other words, luck. Once liberated, survivors were displaced persons, left to remember what happened to their peers and what might have happened to them.

When the Russians finished liberating the camps surrounding Lublin, they placed some 50,000 Jews in camps surrounded by barbed wire. The Jews were safe from persecution, but for some, the guilt of being alive was worse than the daily threat of death they faced in concentration camps. Although relatively few Jews committed suicide while prisoners in the concentration camps, hundreds took their own lives shortly after liberation. By one estimate, as many as sixty suicides occurred each week in the Lublin compound.

Russian treatment of the liberated Jews was for the most part properly humane and sometimes even generous. But loneliness, guilt and the memory of such incredible suffering overwhelmed many of the survivors.

Slowly, the camp victims came back to life. Although Jews were supposed to remain confined to their quarters at Lublin, the Russians allowed many of them to leave the camp site and live on their own. Forming their own "kibbutz" (communal living and work areas), they recalled their experiences, talked among themselves, and made decisions for the future. Part of the talk among Zionist Jews was the formation of a Jewish homeland in Palestine.

Surviving Jews did not forgive their Nazi torturers. Some spent the rest of their days searching out and attempting to kill Nazi soldiers. One Jewish organization, DIN, was very dept at hunting down Hitler's henchmen.

There is a Hebrew phrase, *Dahm Y'Israel Nokeam* which translates, "The blood of Israel will take vengeance"; thus the initials DIN. From 1945 on, members of this organization have sought out Nazi criminals.

DIN drew up a priority list of Nazis who took part in the Jewish slaughter, and systematically sought them out. Working mostly throughout Germany, they divided into specific units, and found contacts which led them to their quarry.

Standard procedure was to drive to the Nazi's home, or stop him on the street, and ask that he report to headquarters for routine questioning. Once taken away the prisoner was driven to a deserted area, where the DIN identified itself, then executed the former Nazi.

Among those the DIN sought out and subsequently killed were:

1. SS Brigadier General Dr. Ernst Grawitz; chief medical officer of the SS; also director of the medical

experimentation program carried out on the women of the Ravensbruch concentration camp.

2. SS Brigadier General Dr. Wilhelm Albert; chief of the Security Police at Lodz. He was also awarded a medal for his part in the final liquidation of the Lodz ghetto in 1944.

In the first two months of the so-called "Jewish hunting season," over 100 participants in mass murder of the Jews were executed by the DIN.

More formal punishment for Nazi war crimes was officially carried out as a result of the formation of the International Military Tribunal at Nuremberg on November 20, 1945. Nazi leaders captured by the Allies were tried for crimes against humanity; especially Jews killed in German concentration camps. Among those tried at Nuremberg were, Hermann Goering, Rudolf Hess, and Hans Frank (Governor General of Occupied Poland). Long before the Nuremberg trials Hitler and Goebbels had already committed suicide.

Six Nazi organizations, defined as criminal, were also on trial at Nuremberg. They were, the Reich Cabinet, the Leadership Corps of the Nazi Party, the SS, the SA, the Gestapo, and the General Staff and High Command of the German Armed Forces.

On Oct. 1, 1946, 12 defendants were sentenced to death, while the others received sentences ranging from life in prison to various jail terms. Three were acquitted. Before he could be executed, Goering committed suicide by taking poison.

Other trials related to Nazi war crimes also occurred between 1946 and 1949. Most of these defendants were accused of committing crimes against concentration camp inmates during the war.

Perhaps the most celebrated trial of a Nazi war criminal was that of Adolf Eichmann, one of the organizers of the *Final Solution;* he was the man who publicly called for the absolute extermination of every Jew on earth.

In 1941 Eichmann was selected by Himmler to assume complete responsibility for the operation against the Jews. From that time until the end of the war Eichmann concerned himself with improving methods of killing Jews and facillitating their execution.

After the war Eichmann eluded capture and finally escaped to Argentina in 1950. While there he once told a Nazi journalist, "...had we killed all of them, the 10.3 million [living in Europe at the time] I would be happy." It has been said by Germans who knew Eichmann that, of all the ruthless Nazis, he was the most callous.

In 1960, after a massive, worldwide manhunt, Eichmann was discovered and brought to Israel for trial. His trial took place in Jerusalem in 1961. Seated in a bullet-proof glass booth, flanked by two armed security guards, Eichmann listened quietly to the charges brought against him.

Literally thousands of documents and hundreds of witnesses were used by the prosecution as proof of Eichmann's role in the extermination of European Jewry. Although Eichmann rarely disputed the evidence, the defense attempted to minimize his actual role in the systematic slaughter of Jews.

Eichmann was convicted by the court of all charges brought against him. In the spring of 1962, he was executed.

If it was difficult for Jews to fully comprehend what was happening to them during the period of deportation to concentration camps, it was equally unimaginable for those who lived outside Nazi-occupied Europe. In April of 1945, several American Congressmen visited Buchenwald. Despite what they had heard regarding German atrocities, they never fully realized its meaning until they looked upon it with their own eyes. Said Representative Henry Jackson, Democrat from Washington State, "We heard atrocity stories which were not verified, but now we have seen them with our own eyes and they are the most sordid I have ever imagined."

Far more Jews than most people imagine fought against the Nazi regime. Some fought as non-Jews under assumed identities. Others fought as part of the Allied armies. Nearly one and a half million Jews represented the United States, Soviet Union, England and other Allies in their fight against the Germans. Another 200,000 Jews, including Eastern European partisans and Palestinians, also worked and fought against the Nazis.

It is also important to remember that those who lived through prison-camp confinement survived, in part, because they were somehow able to maintain their personal sense of humanity, despite the horror of camp life.

Many who lived enoucraged themselves to go on so that, should the time come, they could tell their story. So long as someone lived to tell what those times were like, death would not be in vain.

While some felt guilty for living through the Holocaust, others felt no shame for surviving the most horror in the history of humanity. As one survivor told Terrence Des Pres, author of the book, *The Survivor,* "I feel no guilt in being a survivor, but I feel that I have a task to fulfill." The task he refers to is that of bearing witness to the terrible tragedy of the Holocaust.

On March 12, 1952 the Israeli Foreign Minister Moshe Sharett sent to the governments of France, Britain, U.S.A and U.S.S.R., as the occupying forces of Germany, a note demanding $1.5 billion from both the West and East German governments. The contents of the note reported in David Ben-Gurion's autobiography, *Israel: A Personal History,* said, in part, "A crime of such vast and fearful dimensions as that committed by the Germans in the destruction of one-third of the Jewish people cannot be expiated by any measure of material reparation. All that can be done is to secure the indemnification of the heirs of the victims and rehabilitation of the survivors."

Only the U.S.S.R. did not respond sympathetically to the note. The then West German Chancellor Konrad Adenauer, seven months later said that his government was willing "to arrive at a solution to the problem of material reparations by means of negotiations with representatives of the Government of Israel which has absorbed such a large number of Jewish refugees, and with the representatives of the Jewish people."

A debate in the Knesset began. The Israeli parliament was divided. More than money was at stake. According to Ben-Gurion, one group claimed that "reparations would destroy the nation's moral backbone and spiritual uniqueness." But the greatest objection came from Menachem Begin as spokesman for his Herut party, which had eight members in the Knesset. The money the Government wanted from Germany was, obviously, more than for just reparation (something which admittedly could never be fulfilled) but to bolster its economy. On a most pragmatic basis money from Germany, no matter how deserved in light of the

Holocaust, would provide much-needed funds. Nevertheless, Begin, in a speech to the Knesset, reached an emotional pitch when he claimed that reparations "were the ultimate abomination, the like of which we have not known since we became a nation."

The power of Begin's oratory, the firmness of his mind, the power of his intellect and the drama of his rhetoric can be best judged from this excerpt from that speech:

In Zion Square, to fifteen thousand Jews, I said: "Go, surround the Knesset, as in the days of Rome. When the Roman procurator wanted to set up an idol in the Holy Temple the Jews came from all corners of the country, surrounding the building and said, 'Over our dead bodies!' And to the Knesset I say, there are things in life that are worse than death. This is one of them. For this we will give our lives. We will leave our families. We will say goodbye to our children, but there will be no negotiations with Germany. I know that you have power. You have prisons, concentration camps, an army, a police force, detectives, artillery, machine guns. It makes no difference. On this matter all this force will shatter like glass against rock. I know you will drag me off to a concentration camp. Today you have arrested hundreds. Perhaps you will arrest thousands. We will sit together with them. If necessary we will die together with them but there will be no reparations from Germany.

Menachem Begin was not arrested. Eventually the Government policy won out. The German government entered into negotiations where money and goods would be paid to Jews throughout the world as well as in Israel. The Bundestag ratified the agreement in March of 1953.